YOU CAN DO IT!

Senator Proxmire's Exercise,
Diet and Relaxation Plan

WILLIAM PROXMIRE

SIMON AND SCHUSTER · NEW YORK

RA 776
P868

SBN 671–21576–0 CASEBOUND
LIBRARY OF CONGRESS CATALOG CARD NUMBER: 73–5251
DESIGNED BY EVE METZ
MANUFACTURED IN THE UNITED STATES OF AMERICA

1 2 3 4 5 6 7 8 9 10

MY THANKS TO ARLENE BRANCA FOR TYPING THE MANUSCRIPT.

TO TED, CICI AND DOUGLAS

CONTENTS

VI · DIET

VII · RELAXATION

VIII · PUTTING IT ALL TOGETHER

I· YOUR PHYSICAL CONDITION

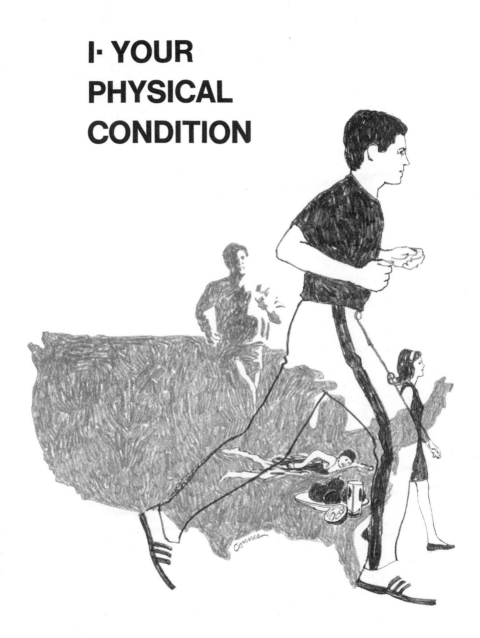

1 · Your Patriotic Duty

A COUNTRY IS no better or worse than its people. With our proud and gallant history, our marvelous resources, our incredibly efficient economic system, and especially our superb constitutional democratic political system, Americans should be blessed as no other people have been in history.

We are the preeminent country in the world and shouldn't feel we have to apologize for it. We are number one in military power, number one in economic abundance, number one in virtually every standard of the good life.

And yet, perhaps in part because of our enviable wealth, we are as a nation in one hell of a mess. The reason is simple: As a people we are a physical wreck. We are too fat, too soft, too tense. We are prone to alcoholism and increasingly to drug addiction. We are lazy. We are thoughtlessly self-indulgent, and unless we get a grip on ourselves, unless we straighten out, we are not long for leadership. We are going to fail and we will deserve to lose what we have. And this soft, fat, tense physical condition of ours is why in spite of all our blessings the world looks so grim, so sad, so boring, so empty to so many of us. A people that relies on booze for a pickup, on cigarettes or a tranquilizer for relaxation, on aspirin to relieve tensions, on sleeping pills for sleep—such a people is not only physically sick but bound to be sad and depressed, to feel that the world—even a good and happy world—is out of joint.

It's Our Fault

The trouble, to paraphrase Shakespeare, is not in our stars but in ourselves—if the world seems sour, the basic remedy lies not in the White House or the halls of Congress but in you and me and every other American. When you're bubbling over with good health, when you're rested and relaxed and know that you can relax fully whenever you will it, when your energy is primed with the right food, when your system is not loaded and fatigued with fat, when you abound with the energy of being in strong physical shape, the world not only looks better—you've made it better.

I have been a vigorous critic of wasteful federal spending. But that isn't our fundamental problem. There is plenty wrong with government and government is my specialty and my responsibility. But there is very little that government as such can or should do to overcome the basic sicknesses that plague America.

The time has come to face up to our responsibility for our own physical well-being. Our world is in danger of imminent pollution. But even more important, we as a people are suffering from a widespread personal pollution. Ecology is the new cry, and that's good. But human ecology is a prime American problem. And in this book my mission is to do something about that need for a better human ecology.

Your Patriotic Duty

You have a personal responsibility, not just to yourself, not just to your family, but to your country, to develop and maintain a sound and healthy body.

No, we should not pass laws to force you to maintain it. We tried that with Prohibition. It didn't work. And government has no business getting into what you do with your body anyway. But if we are going to continue as the proud and great country we have been, we must take a hard look at ourselves—at what we eat, how much we exercise, and how we deal with tension.

That's what this book is all about. And if I leave no other legacy as a senator than this program of what you and two hundred million other Americans can do to get in shape and stay in shape, I will die happy.

Putting It All Together

It's strange that nothing concerns and excites the American people more than books and articles and talks about diet, exercise, well-being. And yet nowhere that I know of is there a really complete book that puts it all together. There are books on running and books on walking, books on swimming, a few books, including Colonel Kenneth Cooper's great *Aerobics*, on overall exercise, but few good books on both exercise and diet.

This book goes even a step beyond that. It not only proposes sound exercise and diet regimes for you, it also proposes something I am sure is about to be discovered by Americans and civilized people everywhere, the new "science" of self-control—that is, relaxing your muscles and mind and emotions at will.

I hope you'll find this book exciting and intriguing. I hope so because if you are going to pay any attention to it, you must enjoy reading it. I think you will.

But I also have the very serious mission of trying to persuade you to adopt the principles of this book to some extent. You don't have to become an exercise nut or a diet nut. But if you read this book and dwell on it, discuss it, think about it, you may begin to become more self-conscious about your body, your obligation to it, not only for your own health and happiness, but for the good of your family, your community, your state, and, yes, your country.

No Reason to Deteriorate with Age

Why are we almost universally in worse shape at thirty than at twenty and worse still at forty than at thirty, and in the end even worse off at fifty—and sixty? Think about it. There is absolutely no reason for this, yet it's accepted as certainly as the sunrise that as we get older our health deteriorates, we have less strength, less stamina, less energy, less vitality. My own experience is that if you exercise regularly and vigorously, eat a moderate and balanced diet, and learn how to relax, you can be in far better shape as you get older than when you were young.

George Bernard Shaw wasn't kidding when he said, "What a pity youth is wasted on the young." Since they have nothing to compare it to, there is no way that most young people can really know and enjoy the immense blessing of their healthy vitality. For the overwhelming majority of young people, this great gift of youth is accepted without appreciation.

In my opinion youth is greatly overrated, especially in America. At forty, fifty, sixty, or older you can have literally all the physical pleasure of youth—the health, the attractive appearance, the vitality and exuberance—and the added satisfaction of awareness. If youth offers anything else, what is it?

Youth is likely to be a period of uncertainty, frustration, and depression. The young are not able to fully savor and reflect on and relax and enjoy good health. On the other hand, with glowing good health, maturity can truly be a happy, joyful, full, exuberant time of life. Truly the best.

Best of Both Ages

If only you could put the best of these two periods of life together—the health and exuberance of youth and the wisdom and maturity of older years!

Well, the Proxmire program enables you to do just exactly that. You don't believe it? Well, try it. Even a vigorous two or three-mile walk every day will start you off right, and when you add more exercise and eat the right amount of the right kind of food and learn how to relax, you'll feel and look better than you have in years. Ponce de León didn't find the Fountain of Youth, but if this program doesn't lead to it, I'd like to know what does!

2 · Your Responsibility for Your Physical Condition

AS A YOUNG MAN just out of college, I once saw an enchanting girl performing in a nightclub. She had everything. She was the most breathtakingly beautiful girl I had ever seen—exquisite features, lovely skin, a radiant smile, and a superb figure. She had one devastating shortcoming. Her voice was a nasal twang. It was flat and irritating.

Because I was taking a series of speech lessons and was working with a remarkably impressive teacher at the Goodman Theatre School in Chicago, I immediately thought how much she would benefit from the school. After the performance I approached the girl and her mother, who was her manager, and said that I would like to make them an interesting proposal. I said that I thought the daughter should attend the Goodman Theatre School for a year. That would mean a full day of classes five days a week. She would work on diction, enunciation, pronunciation, tone, and pitch, and I would pay for it and pay her a salary while she was going to the school.

In return I wanted her to sign a contract in which I would get 50 percent of everything she earned for five years after her year of school and then 10 percent for the next five years. And I pointed out that she would go nowhere without a voice. A voice was what she needed and just about all she needed. Here was a golden chance for her to get it.

Her mother agreed enthusiastically. The daughter said no. She would have to get up early and work all day at the school, and she knew I would break the contract if she didn't live up to it to the letter.

Were My Intentions Honorable?

Maybe you wonder about my relationship with that girl. At the time we were both single and unattached and she obviously had a very strong, exciting physical appeal to me, but we had no dates, no romantic attachment. We never even held hands or shook hands. You may say, Now come on, Senator. Wasn't there something in the back of your mind? There sure was. But as long as that girl had that voice and accent I couldn't stand her. What was in the back of my mind, and as a matter of fact in the front of my mind, was that maybe I could change that voice. Maybe I could create a new and different personality. Maybe then I could fall in love with her. Maybe that was it. But then maybe I was kidding myself. What I really wanted to discover was whether I could find a soul mate who could develop the same kind of drive, self-discipline, personal ambition, desire to improve herself, that I had. But that beautiful young lady said no. She couldn't find it in herself to accept the discipline and the direction, which is what I really wanted.

And I was all wrong anyway. For developing and motivating a personality you should start and end with yourself. You and you alone have the right to determine what kind of person you are going to be. Not even a husband or a wife or a prospective husband or wife really has that right.

Remake Yourself

I tell this story because it illustrates a very common human failing. We've all met people whom we would like to change, improve, perfect. Maybe it's a child, a spouse, a friend. Maybe it's a stranger. When you see someone who has a great potential, but simply lacks a quality that can be inculcated by training, it's very tempting to want to remake this human material.

The question is what right you or I have in a free society to make anyone into what he is not. Our right to remake starts and ends with ourselves. The one person over whom I have or should have full and complete control is myself. I had no right to interfere with that girl's life. And she was undoubtedly right to make her own decision and say no.

The one human being over whom I have unquestionable control and the right to change, modify, adjust, deprive, reward in any way I see fit is myself. And this book is about the program I developed to make those changes.

Like many people, I've been a physical fitness buff most of my life. I really enjoy getting into shape, whether it's exercising, dieting, relaxing, or even trying out some of the new scientific self-discipline contraptions, like controlling your brain waves, your muscular tension, or your temperature.

For this reason I've been delighted to read anything I could get my hands on about health. I'm a pushover for the latest book on how to take care of your heart. I can't resist exercise books, of which Colonel Cooper's *Aerobics* is the best I've come across so far. Almost any kind of diet book I find of some use, especially Adelle Davis' *Let's Eat Right to Keep Fit,* and *Biofeedback,* by Karling and Andrews.

Diet Isn't Enough

The right kind of foods and vitamins can prevent illness, they say. You are what you eat, they say. They also say you replace every cell in your body—you build a new you—every few months. And the kind of new you you build depends on what you put into your mouth.

Does that mean you can eat your way to health? No, because by itself diet just won't do it. You can diet, be the right weight, with all the necessary vitamins and minerals you need, and still be a flabby, weak, tense, irritable, un-healthy organism. You'll be better than you were. But you can still be a mess.

Exercise

And exercise? Exercise can do far more for you than you probably realize. Enough of the right kind of exercise (and most of what is considered exercise is just not the right kind) can make you lean and lithe, even when you continue to eat what you like. It can help you sleep better, clear your mind. An increasing number of doctors now recognize that vigorous daily exercise sessions of at least twenty or thirty minutes without letup can also do wonders in preventing heart disease. It's no guarantee, but it's a big help.

Yet exercise by itself won't do the job either. If you eat too much and too much of the wrong things, if you don't rest enough, if you don't know how to relax, you can exercise ten hours a day and still be tense and unhealthy. You can be an illness-prone athlete. Yes, you can have vitamin deficiency. You can suffer from bad eyesight or bad teeth. Exercise alone is not enough.

Relax

Now—as never before—you can learn to relax. Transcendental meditation is one method. For another, the new biofeedback machines teach you to control your physical and mental tensions. They're going to be the rage in a few years. They'll help you sleep easily and deeply, and they represent a better road to health. But of one thing you can be sure—by themselves they won't do the job. Relax, rest enough, and if you eat the wrong things and fail to exercise you can still be a spongy, soft, flabby, illness-prone, relaxed, and easygoing slob.

Does this mean you can put it all together and come out looking like Ali McGraw or Rock Hudson and always feeling healthy?

No Cure-all

No, this isn't a cure-all. There just isn't any way you and I can stay alive forever. We come into this world with genes that limit our size, our strength, our beauty or ugliness, our intelligence, our capacity to live without disease, and the length of our life. And that's not the end of it. If we grew up in a tense household with mom and dad fighting and hating, if we ate a health-eroding diet in our childhood and youth, if we smoked and drank booze—especially if we did it excessively—if for thirty or forty or fifty or more years we haven't bothered to run or swim or even walk very much—well, that means we have a big job to do.

And of course this means there are limits on what this book and what it proposes can do for you now.

But it can do a lot for you, and for your country too. The most precious resource for any country by far is not its land, its water, its mineral wealth, its factories or farms or military strength. The real resource is its people. And a big element of that resource is the health of its people.

Every year we spend billions of your tax dollars to restore a little of the health damage done by the incredibly unhealthy habits of our modern American life. My good friend and Senate colleague, Ted Kennedy, has written a book saying that we must spend more on health insurance and Medicare.

Political realists say that your tax bill for this too fat, too soft, too sick, too tense people of ours is going to be more and more burdensome as every year passes. Well, that will help. It will ease the pain. It will buy a few extra years. Some of those years will be miserable, some may be good. But no matter how much we spend on Medicare, Medicaid, health care of any kind Congress has yet considered, we will still be a nation of too soft, too sickly people.

Maybe it has to be this way. But this book is my effort to do something about it.

It's Up to You

You are not a helpless victim of your heredity and environment. Do I mean you can be anything you want to be? Of course not. But you'll be astonished if you think about how much you actually can do with yourself.

You can be fatter or leaner.

You can be stronger.

You can be more alert.

You can sleep better.

You can be much more relaxed.

You can feel better, probably much better.

You can almost eliminate colds and headaches.

You can look better: clearer skin, better posture, much better physique—and with plastic surgery, if you have the desire and the money, more hair on your head, a beautiful nose, no bags around the eyes, and fewer wrinkles.

You can have fewer illnesses of almost all kinds and less time in the hospital.

You can probably live a little longer.

So with all this, you can see that you're not a helpless pawn of your environment.

In fact you can create your own version of *My Fair Lady*. You can be Professor Henry Higgins to your own Eliza.

You Face a Long, Tough Grind

This book won't do any of those things for you. This book can only point the way. It won't make it easy for you. There's nothing easy about dieting. It's tough for most of us. And there's nothing easy about the kind of exercise that will do you any clear and lasting good. It can be grueling and dull and tough, but the results should be worth it for you.

There's nothing easy about breaking a lifetime habit of tension and learning to stay with your new relaxed self. You have to pay the price in practice, time, patience, even boredom. Only you can tell whether it's worth it, and the chances are you don't know yet. You'll have to try it for a while; maybe you'll last a day or a week. But if you stay with it, you get more than a better mind and body and personality, you achieve a prime quality for a human being: mastery of self. You won't be the victim of your bad habits. You'll be a freer person than you've ever been.

As a senator devoted to a free society, I can help to pass or repeal laws with the aim of giving us all a freer life. But our biggest share of freedom must come from within us.

Self-Discipline: Price of Freedom

You may now be enslaved by a gluttonous appetite, or a lassitude that prevents you from getting off your behind to exercise, or an habitual anxiety that sometimes keeps you awake and can wear you down to an irritable nag. You're a citizen in a free country, but you're not truly free if you cannot control your own behavior. You're in jail, but this book gives you a key. Okay, you've got the key but turning the lock can be tough for you. It's only hard because the lock is rusty. With patience and a step-by-step program you can free yourself from all those habits that rob you of the fullest sense of life.

You plan. *You* exercise the options. *You* decide what price *you* pay for how long. *You* make the decision.

I hope you will read this book and go to it. Start building the new you. If you do, you'll be better; so will your family and your community and your country. But suppose you have had it with diet and exercise and you like your tensions (yes, some people actually do)—what can you get from this book? Well, you can see how at least one inner-directed person, who also happens to be a United States Senator, thinks—what makes him tick. Maybe you'll get a good laugh or a long yawn. Why not? It's a free country.

3 · Stick with It!

THERE IS JUST no easy way to fitness. When the ads for exercise books or diet programs tell you that you can be healthier without effort or that you can take off ugly pounds without giving up the foods you love, *run, don't walk,* to the nearest exit! They're just not being candid. There is no way you can take off weight without consuming fewer calories than you use. There is no way you can develop firm contours and strong muscles without exercise.

Let's face it—for most of us, it isn't very much fun at all. If health were easy and fun, everybody would be bubbling over with healthful energy. You and I know this just isn't true.

The great majority of Americans are in very bad physical shape, and there is no easy way out of it.

There is a hard and satisfying way out and here's what it takes: It takes a real, often painful, effort to stay with the kind of exercise that will give you the muscle tone, the stamina, the strength, and the resistance to disease which you ought to have. It takes not one spasmodic burst of a day or a week or a month. It takes a willingness to put yourself through difficult discipline every single day. You simply can't build up a kind of storage house of exercise to draw on later. With all the exercising I do, I'm convinced that if I stopped exercising, in six months I'd be just as soft and fat, sickly and tired as if I'd never been in shape.

A Way of Life

Physical fitness has to be a way of life. It will always be tough. It will always be something you don't want to do. It will always be easier for you to stop. It will always be tempting to stop. But you'll have to accept it as something that you do every day.

The same thing is true of eating the right kinds and the right amounts of food. Of course you can indulge yourself occasionally. You can give up one day, maybe even two days, of exercise. Once in a while you can splurge and eat what you know isn't good for you or eat a little too much—and I stress *a little*. But it is hard to get back to sensible eating after overdoing it. It's easier to stay sensible than to try to go back and forth. If you want to be healthy, you have to stay with it.

No-No Section

How many hundreds of ads have you and I read about how easy it is to lose weight? And for some of us it's true. It is easy. What is often hard is not losing weight, but keeping your weight permanently down once you've lost those extra pounds.

I just happen to think that more than half the battle is knowing this, realizing this. I think too few people do. The reason so many people are yo-yos, losing weight and then bouncing right back to their previous plump and unhealthy condition, is that nobody ever told them and they didn't realize that taking off the weight is not the most difficult thing. The difficult problem that stays with you as long as you are a human being, and therefore have to eat to stay alive, is that you have to accept reasonably rigorous diet and retrain your appetite so that you develop the willingness to say—NO. You must develop the determination to cut down on the amount you eat and the kinds of food you eat, and make it a rigorous daily habit.

Once again this is a matter of consistency. It means wise eating habits every single day.

Admit It Will Be Hard for You

There is no secret to this. The idea is easy and simple to understand. But the execution is very difficult and almost none of the diet books, diet columns, diet articles, or dietitians will tell you the truth. It's hard. In many ways it's far harder to keep on the right diet than it is to give up cigarettes, liquor, or drugs. All those things you can give up totally. With food you can't do that. Every day, probably three times a day, you eat. Every day you are tempted. How many of the millions of people who have succeeded in giving up the cigarette habit would be able to do so if every day they had to smoke cigarettes three times?

How many of those who have stopped drinking could give up liquor if every day they took three drinks at five- or six-hour intervals?

For those of us who like good food, and that includes the overwhelming majority of the human race, this means doing something which is tough and difficult, and the first step toward success is to recognize just exactly that. Once we have done this, once we have recognized the degree of determination and length of determination and the amount of patience and persistence that it will take for us to win, we can be on our way.

At least we make the determination knowing exactly what we're doing. We intend to take off weight, and this is not a resolution for a year—this is a resolution for good.

Self-Discipline, Road to Relaxation

The same principle applies to self-control in learning systematic relaxation. This isn't easy, and unlike exercise and diet, as I point out in a later chapter, it can be very expensive, especially if you buy an EMG and EEG machine that will enable you to monitor your muscular tension and your brain waves until you know just when and how you've relaxed.

But above all, it will take practice, daily, unrelenting practice.

It will take a pattern of living in which, when you go to sleep at night, you go through the full panoply of muscular relaxation, you let go, slow down, and surrender to sleep deliberately in a calculated and disciplined way.

Freedom Through Discipline

I feel that self-discipline of this kind is the way to freedom, freedom from self-destructive habits. By accepting responsibility for ourselves we gain a sense that we are free to be the people we want to be. We don't always admit it, but freedom always requires discipline. Even so, I can easily see how some people might disagree and might question spending so much time, energy, and effort on exercise, diet, and planned and programmed relaxation. If you do all that, they might say, doesn't your freedom disappear?

I think it's a question of how we use our free will. If you use self-discipline to achieve health and fitness, you'll have an inner sense of freedom, but you alone make the free choice.

What this book tries to do is tell you as honestly as possible what that choice means.

Of course I can only tell you how it looks from my vantage point, which is different from yours. But that insight may help you to get a better idea of what it takes to succeed, and to give yourself the fitness and the control to enable you to determine your future.

Improve with Age

When I say you can be in better shape in maturity—in your forties, fifties, sixties—than you were between fifteen and twenty-five, which is considered the prime of physical life, it is based on my own experience.

I can recall vividly trying to run at a steady and regular speed for more than a mile or so when I was in college, or to swim more than fifty yards. I was in better physical condition than most college students, but I simply couldn't do it. And I can remember the infinite fatigue that would stay with me literally for three or four days after I'd had only five or six hours of sleep for a night or two.

At fifty-seven, after eight years of hard, prolonged exercise and after a deliberately limited diet that has reduced my weight, I find that I have far better endurance than I did in high school or college, that I can run much longer and farther without being tired. I'm sure, for instance, that I would not have been able to run five miles when I was a freshman or a junior or a senior in college without being tired. Now it's no problem. I can swim half a mile or a mile without being significantly fatigued, and when I get only three or four hours of sleep at night, I still feel vigorous and rested. Altogether, I really am far more vigorous, rested, and vital than I was when I was younger.

And, of course, learning how to relax has greatly increased my composure and I'm sure it will yours.

I don't mean to say that getting old even with this kind of program is all clover. But what is? It's true that as you get older there are a few more aches and pains. But those aches and pains are slight and moderate if you have taken good physical care of yourself. To be fully alive now is the important thing, and by being fit we can savor the happy, the sweet, and the good.

II· EXERCISE

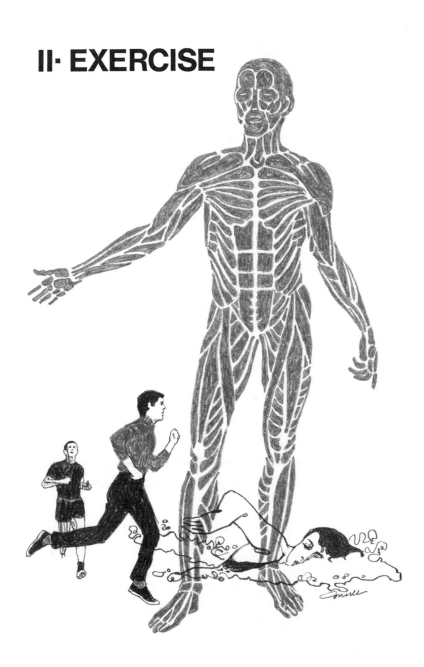

4 · Why Exercise?

FOR MANY, many people almost any kind of exercise is a real drag. And it's true that it is difficult at times to force our muscles to move, especially in a sustained way, and it's this sustained exercise that is most beneficial. But there can be real joy in exercise. There is the sense of increased vitality and the pleasure that comes from feeling and looking fit, along with the dividends of better health, better disposition, and longer life.

If you exercise enough you will be leaner, stronger, more energetic. You'll love life, enjoy the smell of flowers, the taste of your food, the cold, and the bracing freshness of a morning breeze. You can literally exercise your way out of boredom, listlessness, anxiety. I will tell you how to do it.

And you'll look so much better. The heavy jowls, the sagging stomach, the yellowish or pallid complexion will diminish and then vanish with exercise. Exercise won't grow hair on your head, alas. And it won't give you the nose you want, won't make you taller, won't change your bone structure. But it will do just about everything else and everything else is plenty. It will put a warm, pink color in your cheeks. It will eliminate the bulges and sags and fat. It will put firmness in your muscles, put a brightness in your eye.

All this is true because the essence of good looks is simply good health. The most pitiful-looking people on earth are the least healthy. When a man or woman is unhealthy and out of shape, he or she has bad color and skin, a misshapen body, hunched-over posture, and many other ugly side effects. When he or she is glowing with health, the total appearance is attractive. It's that simple.

You'll sleep better, much better, with exercise. You may live longer. Your prospects of suffering the number-one killer, heart disease, will be reduced. And your resistance against almost any other kind of illness will be sharply improved.

Your Body Made to Exercise

Think of it this way. Mankind evolved over at least a million, perhaps two million, years—that is, mankind as you and I know it today, with faces and bodies like ours and brains very much like our brains.

Now think what one million years means. Allowing twenty-five years to a generation, it means *40,000* generations! You and I can't envision what that means, but if you listed the first name of each of your 40,000 ancestors going back for a million years, at two hundred words to a page, they would cover the next two hundred pages!

Now why do I bring all this up? Because every one of those 40,000 ancestors of yours down to the last five or ten spent almost all his life exercising almost all the time.

The reason he wasn't beautiful, vibrant, with *joie de vivre,* in spite of all that exercise, was because up until a few hundred years ago life was nasty, brutish, and short. If your ancestors had had the vitamins, the food, the rest, and the other advantages that you and I have, they could have been and would have been a super race—handsome, sparkling with personality, mentally bright and quick. But they didn't have our advantages and in terms of exercise we certainly don't have theirs.

Now we have the chance to put it all together. Almost no human beings these days exercise even 5 or 10 percent as much as they should to develop their physical potential. Because our body evolved through tens of thousands of generations of people shaped by hard physical exercise, it is ready for it, built for it, and is now having a miserable time adjusting to a life of physical indolence. This is the reason for the heart-disease epidemic which has burst on this generation as plague and famine burst on previous generations. This is why we've become a soft and fat, lazy, dyspeptic, miserable people.

The exercise section of this book will tell you how you can overcome this soft indolence in the course of your everyday life, and how to do it in a systematic, disciplined way that costs what you want to spend in time, effort, and discomfort. And the book as a whole shows you how to complement your exercise with diet and rest. A disciplined exercise program can give you a happier body to live in, which means a warmer disposition and a more alert intelligence to go along with it.

You Are the Work You Do

There is a truism that we are what we do, that the job a man does in life makes him what he is. Dull, repetitive, automatic, assembly-line work dulls and slows your senses. A lively, demanding job keeps you alert. It is possible to retain a sharp and sensitive intelligence after years of doing nothing with it, but it's not easy. Over the years your brain or the force of your personality gradually loses its capacity for action if it lies fallow in disuse.

Of course the job isn't everything. The job itself can be dull, but the social give-and-take at the office, factory, or at home and with your friends may provide the necessary challenge and provocation for individuals to develop.

For almost all the million years and 40,000 generations since mankind has inhabited this planet, that didn't matter. Hard, long physical activity was work. Man *had* to do this kind of work to live, to eat, to shelter and clothe himself, to protect and nourish his family. He had to hunt for long, arduous days, he had to toil in the field.

Even as recently as a hundred years ago, the sedentary man frequently walked miles to or from work, moved ceaselessly around his store, lifting and climbing, and then walked miles home to pump water, chop wood, repair his house. And he was *sedentary!*

The Hardhat, a Softie?

Today even the manual worker leads a far softer, easier life, with little or no physical activity. He rides to work, sits most of the day in a crane or a truck or presses buttons or pushes levers on a machine. Yet he is the manual worker. He is viewed in our society as a man who uses his muscles, he's the hardhat, the blue-collar worker. Of course some hardhats and other blue-collar workers still do difficult physical work, but far fewer than in the past.

Even farmers now spend more time sitting on their tractors or other farm equipment, letting the machine work for them, rather than in actual prolonged physical effort.

The housewife of a couple of generations ago labored physically for hours preparing meals, cleaning the house with a broom and a dust cloth, walking to and from the store, lugging the family groceries. Today she probably does much more actual physical work than her husband, but far, far less than her grandmother did. With all the household labor-saving gadgets, and the family car, physical activity has been dramatically reduced.

And the kids! Talk about school busing! What's wrong with letting a healthy child walk two or three miles or even more to school and home again? It would do him a world of good. But next to the sin of stuffing our children with food by forcing them to clean their overloaded plate at every meal, the next most common crime we as parents commit against their health is driving them to school or insisting that the school bus stop at every corner.

It's no surprise to me that in a recent contest between teenage girls and women in their seventies, a contest that included races and other physical activities, the women in their seventies swept to a consistent triumph over their granddaughters.

What a lifetime of health our children miss by not walking a few miles to and from school every day!

TV—the Indolent Life

Every member of the family suffers from a passivity in the entertainment and diversions of today.

Even our dancing is passive. Contrast the old square dances and polkas, with their rousing, boisterous activity, to modern dances in which a young man and woman stand on the floor, separated but facing each other, languidly moving hands and arms and remaining in one spot.

But dancing could have a great future. Sonny Rooker, the dynamic head of the Texas Physical Fitness Program, tells me that Jackie Sorensen, a physical-fitness specialist in Atlanta, Georgia, is introducing "aerobic" dancing into physical-fitness programs, to the joy and delight of physical fitness buffs.

Miss Sorensen has developed dances that last twenty or thirty uninterrupted minutes, that are sufficiently fast paced so that they are the equivalent of a vigorous walk, or preferably of jogging.

With all the delightful motivations dancing combines—interchange, sexual association—this could be a combination of exercise and relaxation that will make a significant difference in the physical-fitness level of our country. And what a great way to become physically fit!

It would be wonderful to get back to active entertainment. Consider the appalling lassitude of an entire country where more time is spent sitting or lying before a television set than in any other activity except working and sleeping. It's almost an addiction, and I think for some people it is a drug.

Even our most popular sports—baseball, golf, fishing—do

not require any prolonged activity that is of value to the heart or circulatory system.

The point I want to stress is that *active work makes the man.* Lack of physical work gradually destroys him physically. Machines—the automobile, the tractor, and a variety of machine tools—end up doing our physical work. The result is a fat, lazy, sick people.

This is why we need a planned program of self-enforced physical activity. We need this activity not only for the few years we are schoolchildren, but for a lifetime.

What Can Exercise Do?

There are all kinds of reasons for exercise. Some of us exercise to feel better, some to look better, some to be able to eat more, some to be able to sleep or relax more easily, some undoubtedly just for the sheer joy of exercise and the feeling of well-being that follows it.

Perhaps one of the least common reasons to exercise is to prevent disease. However, such a motivation is increasingly supported by medical experts and may well become a major part of preventive medicine programs.

Many heart specialists, including the great Dr. Paul Dudley White, advocate gradually developing a program of prolonged vigorous exercise. They have offered thoughtful expert analysis of precisely why exercise of this kind will reduce the likelihood of heart attacks.

But the most exciting possibility to me is in the still-to-be-explored areas of preventive medicine. I don't know of any medical expert who will state that vigorous exercise is likely to inhibit the occurrence of cancer, although I have read some research findings of great interest in this area. Obviously the work in this field must be subjected to a great deal more investigation, experimentation, and analysis before it can be accepted, but it is interesting to consider the possibility that vigorous exercise could inhibit cancer.

A few years ago a group of scientists experimenting with rats found that a substance formed in the process of muscle fatigue hampers the growth of animal cancer. Rats allowed to exercise freely proved more resistant to the growth of transplanted cancer than rats kept inactive in small individual cages. Inhibition of cancer growth was even more marked in animals forced to do strenuous exercise, such as running for many miles each day in a labyrinth or swimming for hours in a tank. When the bodies of the rats were analyzed it was found that those forced to lead completely indolent lives had carried cancers five to ten times the weight of those that were forced to exercise strenuously.

According to Dr. Carl E. Paschkis, director of the Division of Endocrin and Cancer Research at Jefferson Medical College in Philadelphia, in some cases the cancer in the exercised rats seemed to have disappeared completely. The most important discovery from the research point of view, Dr. Paschkis announced, was the fact that cancer growth was also markedly inhibited in animals injected with the by-product of muscle fatigue. The exact nature of the active ingredient produced in rat muscle fatigue is still unknown.

The amount of exercise those rats underwent was prodigious. They were running for twelve hours a day or swimming daily for three or four periods of two or three hours each. This amount of exercise seems so extreme that the experiment may not sound encouraging to a layman, but scientists consider it an important finding.

What this experiment suggests is not that exercise will prevent or cure cancer, but that there may be a significant difference in the incidence of cancer and the killing effect of cancer between, on the one hand, the life of virtual indolence and, on the other hand, the life of very, very vigorous exercise.

At any rate, here is another reason for a program of long, vigorous exercise. It just might—and, of course, this is an outside chance—help to prolong or save your life.

The Happy Pay-off—Vitality and Confidence

It's amazing how the body reacts to continuous vigorous exercise. It becomes lean, strong, lithe, responsive. The very fact that you are able to walk or run much farther without being tired, or to swim for a longer period without fatigue, means that you can carry on any other kind of activity with greater vigor and without the increasing pain of exhaustion. Even during extended periods of hard work, fatigue comes much later, more slowly, and touches you more lightly.

You'll find that vitality wells up in you. At the same time it's easier to relax, sleep is more natural and easy. Your resistance to disease is sharply improved. And, of course, disease is a major cause of aging and premature death.

As you develop a strong, resilient body, you also develop a happy confidence. For many people, feelings of inadequacy grow out of their feelings of physical weakness. They are easily tired and unhappy about their lack of physical fitness.

No doubt a lack of stamina and physical self-assurance has led many people to give up and accept defeat in work and many other areas of life. They just don't think they are good enough physically. The genuine physical strength and endurance provided by vigorous prolonged exercise, sound diet, and relaxation are a solid basis for overcoming this lack of confidence.

5 · The Painful Joy of Exercise

IT'S JONATHAN LIVINGSTON SEAGULL versus Robert Maynard Hutchins.

Who is Jonathan Seagull? If you haven't read the best-selling book about him, you should. Jonathan couldn't have cared less about what other seagulls live for—scrounging, spearing, snatching food. He flatly rejected all that.

Jonathan's cup of tea was a soaring, diving, twisting flying speed. He practiced and practiced hour after hour, day after painful day, usually far into the night, until he could turn, barrel roll, Immelmann at more than seventy miles an hour.

And dive! Jonathan would climb to almost a mile in the sky and dive at a screeching, one hundred, one fifty, and then more than two hundred miles an hour. For his kind of daring Jonathan suffered exile from his fellow seagulls. But he broke free of the ordinary and through discipline learned things no seagull had learned before. It's a great story.

And who is Robert Maynard Hutchins? Hutchins is a renowned scholar who at the tender age of thirty became the youngest president of a major university in the country when he took over the University of Chicago. Intellect, personality, prestige—Hutchins has them all. He also has a rather extreme view of exercise: "I never run when I can walk. I never walk when I can stand still. I never stand when I can sit down. I never sit when I can lie down. Whenever I feel the urge to exercise I lie down until it goes away."

Probably most of us fall somewhere between Hutchins and Jonathan Seagull. We want the rewards of exercise but haven't developed the determination to do it regularly. And make no mistake, it takes a considerable amount of that Jonathan Seagull determination to really break through into the joy of vigorous, strenuous, tiring, painful, all-out exercise.

Hanging in There

Overcoming the ordinary inertia or laziness that makes us all want to avoid exercise takes some doing. The body wants to stop but looking toward the goal drives us on. It seems that each of us has enough of the Jonathan Livingston Seagull spirit to master the part of us that resists physical fitness.

After only three lengths in the pool your arms ache and your chest hurts with strain. Your stomach tires with the pull and your lungs never seem to get enough air. You have thirty-three lengths to go. You stay with it. The pain eases some, but it doesn't go away entirely. It's only after a period of regular daily exercise that we begin to see the satisfying results that make these efforts worthwhile.

Jonathan shot down toward the earth at a fantastic two hundred miles an hour. We can't do that. But consider what you can do when you walk, then swing into a lope, then really blaze into an all-out sprint. For a few seconds you're the world's fastest human. Then you cut and dodge. You're zipping through a broken field, dazzling would-be tacklers. You're Dallas' Bob Hayes or Green Bay's John Brockington. You straighten out and zip across the street. You're Maury Wills stealing second on Johnny Bench's great arm.

Yes, you have your moments in running, but if it's going to help your heart and your circulatory system, running is 90 percent steady, relentless, often painful plodding along. What can motivate you to develop a regular program of running or any other strenuous exercise?

First there's the established physiological benefit. This *is* the way to train your body. You do strengthen your heart. You do develop stronger and bigger alternative circulatory channels for your blood stream. You do get stronger. You get stronger exactly as you press on with your tired muscles when they say, No, let's quit. That's the crucial time when the fat melts, the sinews strengthen.

But this isn't all. There's a psychic challenge and reward too. The body has a definite degree of strength and endurance. It can be measured, tested, proven. But the psyche, the will—can that be strengthened?

Here's one vote that says yes. Call it determination or guts or drive, the good distance man has the capacity to go out and seek the pain of prolonged physical exertion and stay with it. Long-distance swimming or running develops the psyche that way.

Strengthen the Will?

Does this really mean that the physical endurance man has a stronger will—or more power of self-discipline? I don't know. It probably depends on many other elements. But *if* his exercise is strictly voluntarily motivated from within, I think it probably does.

The will that brings the distance man through his physical ordeal also gives him the strength to stay with a detailed, boring, complex problem that must be patiently and painfully broken down and analyzed to be understood. And there's a quality to that masochistic discipline that is right at the crux when you resist that tempting combination of delicious food available and waiting—when your system cries for food and the hunger gnaws. It's similar to the tough self-denial required when you know you must relax—let go—drift—and yet those sex or ego fantasies intrude and won't let go. The strong psyche, strengthened by tests of will, can let those fantasies drift away and does.

Prolonged physical exertion requires an inner discipline—

like the psychic chemistry that gives you the will to win with your diet or win in controlling your heartbeat or pulse with relaxation.

Persistence

But the real problem in establishing a program of exercise is not starting it but continuing it. There are probably more failures among those who have determined that they will run a certain amount every day or walk a certain amount every day than there are among dieters. And heaven knows the overwhelming majority of people who try to diet won't stay with it and their weight comes back to its previous level of obesity.

"Try It—You'll Like It"

Now all this may discourage you. Don't let it. First ask yourself: How much do I want to be healthy and happy and relaxed? If you want it even a little, you can have it—not by developing any supermotivation or surpassing will, but by simply taking the time to develop the daily habit of exercise—and believe me you can grow to like it. Sure there will be moments when you look for excuses to avoid it, but not only will the pleasure of exercise exceed the pain, but the side effects—ah, there's the pay-off.

Let me repeat again: You'll sleep better—much better. You'll look better—a lot better. You're sure to feel better. Laughter comes more often, more easily. You're more composed and relaxed, so your kids, your husband or wife, the people you see who bug you—just don't bother you. You can literally laugh them off.

Motivation Can Be Soft and Gentle

I repeat all this because motivation is everything. You don't need what it takes to be an athlete or a thinker or an exciting personality. All you need to be *sure* to succeed is to want to be healthy badly enough so you make the relatively easy and simple sacrifices necessary to achieve health.

Not even your motivation has to be super. If you want to be healthy just enough to walk at a brisk pace for a continuous half-hour every day, you're on your way.

Habit Your Helper

What will make it easier for you is developing the habit. And walk *every* day—not every other day—certainly not when you feel like it or can fit it in, but *every* day. Establishing your habit is the name of the game. This will make health a whale of a lot easier.

Some people have the will or the motivation to exercise three or four days a week—every week. I don't. Why? Because unless the walk is an everyday habit, which is the essential key to successful exercise, you probably won't stay with it. I can tell you now that if you can just get in the habit of taking a modest amount of exercise every day, you will be on your way.

Tips

If you don't have a half-hour that you can spare out of your busy day, here are some tips:

1. Walk *part* of the way to work. And don't tell me that's impossible until you try it. Chances are that you'll save on parking if you leave your car a couple of miles from where you work and walk the rest of the way. Subtract the time it would take you to drive all the way from the half-hour it takes you to walk a couple of miles, and you'll find you have to leave for work just a little earlier and arrive home just a little later.

2. If that still won't work, get up half an hour earlier. Morning is probably the most delightful time of the

day for walking. The outdoors is at its freshest and brightest.

3. Go to bed a little later and walk just before you hit the hay. You'll sleep better and you probably won't need as much sleep.

4. Walk all or part of the way to and from shopping.

5. Walk your dog.

6. If you're younger, walk to and from school or part of the way.

You Can Do It

I have many other suggestions later in the book. But at this point I want to encourage you to recognize that this health kick is really for you. It's easy. You can do it and you'll be a better person because you did.

I've said nothing in this chapter about those of you who prefer jogging or running (there is a difference) to walking, or swimming or even prolonged dancing to either one, or who believe that exercise should be a social occasion with friends or family. All that comes later, and that too, of course, may or may not make it easier and more pleasant.

We're all different. But whatever your inclination, if you want to be as happy and relaxed as good health can make you, recognize that developing a habit of regular daily exercise can take you a long, long way along that route. And you can have a ball in the process.

Take It Easy—at First

Maybe this walking routine is too easy and bland for you. Maybe you think it's pabulum when you want some red meat. You may want to run or at least jog—to get a good, solid, long daily workout, not just a breezy walk. If so that's great, and later chapters are really for you.

But remember that every kind of safe exercise routine must be built on a sound, healthy heart and a good general physical condition—certified by medical examination. Then you gradually work up to the regime you want.

Recently I saw a man at least seventy-five pounds over-weight, with a sagging paunch, jogging painfully around a football field. He was sweating, straining, gasping for air. He kept at it, lap after lap. I admired his drive and will. But I feared for his life the way I'd fear for that of a child chasing a ball into fast-moving traffic. Jogging could kill that man any minute. First he needed to diet off thirty or forty pounds, and meanwhile to confine his exercise to walking a mile at a clip or even a little less.

More of this later. For now just recognize that you can do it. You'll like it. It's easy. You can be fat or thin, young or old, male or female.

Whether you're inclined toward Jonathan Seagull or Dr. Hutchins, exercise *is* for you.

III· WALKING

6 · Walking for Pleasure and Health

WALKING CAN BE a great joy. You can walk any-time, anywhere, under any conditions, and with virtually no equipment. You can amble, stroll, saunter, pace, or stride as disposition moves you. The important thing is to get out and walk!

Of course all of us walk, whether we walk for exercise or not. Very few people walk less than half a mile a day and very few walk more than two or three miles. This is usually broken into short strolls, and few people walk at a pace which provides the kind of exercise that can tone the muscles, improve stamina and endurance, bring color to the cheeks, take off weight, and generally give the zest that exercise can give.

Vigorous Walking a Cultivated Taste

Regular vigorous walking is usually an effort—like work. It isn't fun at first. Probably many people consider it a boring form of exercise, with none of the bounce they associate with splashing in the water, hitting a golf or tennis ball, playing catch with their children, riding a wave with a surfboard, or water skiing. However, once you've started a regular program of walking, you'll be amazed at the pleasure and satisfaction it can bring you. It's a culti-vated taste, like avocados or artichokes.

You have to walk regularly, develop your stamina, stay

with it. You may have to take off weight to really enjoy walking. If you're light and thin, walking can be an easy, happy breeze.

But fat or skinny, strong or weak, if you keep walking you will soon find it close to the top of your pleasures. Walking along on a brisk, cool day with the sun shining, breezes blowing, air filled with the fragrance of grass or leaves or flowers, can be a very pleasant physical experience indeed.

Challenging the Elements

Walking can be satisfying even in bad weather if your clothes are old enough or you have a good raincoat and hat. Rain splashing on your face and hands can be a pleasant experience; it reminds me of happy days in my boyhood.

Walking in a snowstorm with cool, light flakes of snow on your face, with a pad of packed snow underfoot, the fragrance of cold, clean, white, frosty air in your lungs, can be a joy.

And yes, walking in the heat of a humid 90-degree day in Washington with the sweat coursing down your face, under your arms, down your back can also be a pleasant experience if you have developed the stamina and strength that steady walking gives you. No newcomer to exercise should attempt this, but when you are a seasoned walker you'll find that after a while perspiration provides you with your own moderating, cooling system.

I've said nothing about what you can see while you're walking, what you can hear while you're walking, very little about what you can smell while you're walking. I want to mention some of those things later.

There is sheer joy just in the animal pleasure of moving along under your own steam and power, stretching, relaxing, using your body. The good Lord meant it to be used.

Walking and Health

From the standpoint of health, walking is it!

Experts disagree about the value of almost every other kind of exercise—sometimes about whether it has any value and sometimes about whether the activity is likely to be excessive. Some doctors oppose running or even jogging (a slower-paced form of running) on the ground that it may be a strain to the system, particularly for older men and women and especially if it's not done on a daily basis. But every doctor I've ever read about or heard of will agree that walking is as safe an exercise as one can engage in.

Because we walk from the time we are about a year old it is a familiar exercise, and because even a rapid walk can be sustained literally for hours without exhaustion by most healthy people, it is almost by definition a moderate exercise. At the same time it puts all the big muscles of the body into play. When you walk and when you stride, your leg muscles are not the only ones that get a vigorous workout. The muscles of your hips, stomach, chest, shoulders all have to take part.

If you really want to condition your system, if you really want the full benefit to your heart, your lungs, your circulatory system that walking can give—that is, the aerobic benefit of walking, which Dr. Cooper wrote about—then you need a striding, vigorous, steady pace of more than three miles an hour for forty-five minutes or an hour every day.

You won't strain your heart, provided you are reasonably careful about it. That means that it would be wise to have a medical examination before you start a vigorous walking routine. You should also build up gradually to the recommended forty-five minutes by walking maybe ten or fifteen minutes every day for the first week. Then add five minutes each week until you get to forty-five minutes or a full hour.

Relieving Tension

The general physical effects aren't all. There's also a clearly improved sense of well-being that comes as you develop the ability to walk long distances without tiring. You feel stronger, and you are. You sleep better because you're physically tired and relaxed, feel far less tense and nervous. I've also found that since I have walked five miles a day headaches have disappeared. Headaches are usually a matter of tension. That daily hour of relaxation and pleasant unwinding which you get from a long walk relieves your tension for many hours.

All this will give you the relaxation that enables you to concentrate more easily. I have found that since I started my long walks I feel a greater sense of composure and have a relaxed, easy approach that I could not sustain before.

Emotions

There's also an emotional benefit in walking. The next time you feel angry, frustrated, tense, irritable, instead of taking aspirin, a tranquilizer, or a shot of whiskey, take a walk, preferably a long walk. You'll find that a walk is a far greater benefit to your nerves and your emotions than any artificial calmer-downer. It's hard to stay angry or upset when you take a long walk. There are so many things to distract your mind, so many little events that happen in the course of your walk. There's the wind and the sun, or the moon and the stars, or the rain or the snow or the traffic or the smiles or waves of people or the barking dogs.

And then there's the soothing passage of time. You've left an emotional, tense situation with your office colleagues, or your spouse or your children or your parents or your friends, and permitted the soothing perspective of time to work its will.

Walking Fatigue Away

The most surprising physical aspect of walking is the energizing effect. This contradicts everything I expected of walking, and it's a mystery to me why it takes place. I can start off tired and weary at the end of a long day in the Senate, with all kinds of frustrations, feeling too tired to sleep and far too tired to walk, and after that first difficult quarter- or half-mile, not only does the frustration ease but, after my vigorous striding begins, I begin to feel more rested and then fully alert. The reason may be physical or psychological or emotional or all three, but the feeling is definite and clear.

This is something that comes with practice, because until you've walked a great deal your body simply can't stand more than fifteen minutes or half an hour of vigorous hard walking without becoming tired. However, after you have walked a great deal, fifteen minutes to half an hour is very easy. This is because your tiredness is often not a physical matter, it's a matter of the mental and emotional strains you've been under, and so as you walk, the energy begins to pulse back into your system.

Walking the Pounds Off

Another delightful aspect of long walks is that they enable you to lose weight without eating any less. A health study I recently read pointed out that a five-mile walk at a good rate of speed—that is, three and a half to four miles an hour—uses up approximately 400 calories.

What a happy dividend! You spend a very pleasant hour or hour and fifteen minutes relaxing, and instead of having to pay a price, you have the happy reward of eating more without gaining.

At that rate, ten days of this kind of walking will take off a full pound.

And if you say that ten days or fifty miles of walking is a great deal of walking to take off a pound, put it in the framework of a year. If you took off a pound every ten days this way, you would take off thirty-six pounds in the course of a year.

Recently I took off fifteen pounds this way over a four-month period. I did it without reducing my caloric intake below 2,000 calories on any day during that period. I felt very well indeed, but I must say I did more than simply walk five miles. In addition I ran five miles. During a couple of the months I had access to an indoor pool and swam half a mile a day. But I could have taken off the same number of pounds in a slightly longer period without any additional exercise except that vigorous daily five-mile walk.

Walking as a Cure for Tendonitis

Surprising as it may sound, a walk back from my office can greatly ease the tendonitis that afflicts me as a fifty-seven-year-old runner. It seems that tendonitis is endemic to men over forty-five who run a great deal, especially if they run on hard pavements and fairly fast.

Dr. Cooper, the aerobics specialist, told me that all kinds of treatments had been tried to alleviate this problem, none with much success. Then a couple of years ago I read about an English athlete who had crossed the United States in about sixty days. He said that after a couple of days of running he had great difficulty with his tendons. Instead of running the next couple of days, he walked.

One would think that walking, which uses the feet and legs and tendons, would simply aggravate the strain that running produces. But just like that runner, I've found that walking when my tendons are sore seems to heal them to a very considerable degree.

Walking for Long Life

One of the great things about walking is that it's something you can do at any age. How proud and happy we are when a baby takes his first steps. Walking is a supreme accomplishment for all of us when we are toddlers. It's a great achievement. And when we get old we can pace along the same way.

Think about it. Isn't it true that most of the people you know who are in their eighties or nineties have two characteristics in common? One is that they are slender. And the second is that they do a great amount of walking.

Older people attribute their long lives to many different things, but by far the most common characteristic is that they are great walkers. This is equally true of such famous men as Supreme Court Justice Earl Warren and Senator Theodore Francis Green, and of men and women who are respected simply as village elders.

7 · The Proxmire Walking Program

MOST OF WHAT PASSES for walking simply won't do. It's true that any kind of ambling, sauntering, or strolling—anything, as long as you're moving—will probably give you some benefit. It helps speed up the consumption of calories a little and gives you a little muscle conditioning. But the benefits will be very few indeed unless you walk at a reasonably brisk pace. Ideally you should stride at more than three miles an hour, and if possible at four.

You'll be surprised at how fast a walk of three and a half to four miles an hour is. Most people overestimate their walking speed. I'd say the usual rate is about two and a half miles an hour, so you can see that three and a half miles an hour is a good fast walk.

Walking Posture

It helps, though it is not essential, to walk with a good posture. In another part of this book we'll discuss the importance of posture for conditioning, but here let's talk about posture for walking. You'll feel better, look better, move better, and the results will be better if you do the following:

1. Walk tall. That means stretch out, stretch your neck, walk as if you're carrying a bundle of clothes on your head. We often see pictures of women from other cultures who are walking with large burdens on their heads, and they

almost always have superb posture. And that's the way you should walk—stretch your neck, stretch out your back muscles. You can add an inch or two to a slouched posture by simply stretching out.

2. Throw your shoulders back. I have found that the easiest way to achieve the right posture is to stand with your arms extended at your sides and open your palms outward. That slouchy, round-shouldered look disappears and shoulders move back smartly. At the same time pull your stomach in and let your chest go out. You know, most of us are afraid to be a little chesty. I find that whether people are politicians, businessmen, stenographers, or house-wives, they all seem to feel there's something immodest about throwing their chests out and pulling their stomachs in. I am not sure how this idea arose but it couldn't be more false. A proud and graceful carriage is a beautiful sight in women and men.

3. Relax. You'll look better, you'll feel better. I suggest that it's possible to walk tall, with shoulders back, chest out, stomach in, and still be relaxed. Yes, and also to be relaxed while you're moving at a striding, driving speed. You may say, You're putting me on—how can I relax when I have to move faster than is comfortable, stand straighter than is comfortable, stand taller than is comfortable, have my shoulders back more than is comfortable, pull my stomach in more than is comfortable, throw my chest out more than is comfortable? Well, it is more difficult to relax at first, but only at first. With practice—daily practice is best—you'll find yourself relaxing more and more.

The best way to relax with all this is to smile and follow the advice of that ragtime song that says, "If you can't say anything real nice, it's better not to talk at all is my advice." If you can't think of anything that's happy and pleasant and relaxing, just let your mind go, empty your thoughts, and think of nothing but the fact that you are relaxing. The section of the book on relaxation will help greatly, and believe me, the suggestions made there should not simply be applied when you're immobile. They're even more important when you're exercising and moving.

Walk Fast

By far the most important part of the prescription for walking, for aerobic conditioning, is your walking speed. If you walk more than three miles an hour the rest will pretty much take care of itself. As time goes on you'll find yourself improving your posture to maintain the pace comfortably. If you walk at more than three miles an hour you're going to be walking yourself into condition.

In his best-selling book, *Aerobics,* Dr. Kenneth Cooper offers an intriguing formula for desirable walking rates. If you walk less than three miles an hour, Cooper gives you no point credits for aerobic conditioning unless you walk at least two miles. Even if you walk five or ten miles, the points you get on the Cooper Aerobic Chart are only half as great if you walk less than three miles an hour than if you walk more than three miles an hour.

If you walk a little more than four miles an hour, which is very fast indeed, Cooper doubles the points you get for walking at four miles an hour or less. That means if you can stride along at four and a half miles an hour you can get literally four times as much out of it as if you amble along at the usual two and a half.

Of course you get another dividend from walking fast. You cover the distance from your home to your office or from where you park your car to your office in much less time.

Walk, Don't Run

It is possible to get more out of walking than out of jogging, but to do this you have to be a real heel-and-toe man. Perhaps you have seen those pictures on television or in the movies of Olympic walkers who cover seven miles in an hour, which is actually a faster rate than the usual jogging rate. It is considered walking only because both feet are on the ground at the same time. But the feet move very fast indeed and the arms, instead of moving loosely at the sides, come up slightly so the fists swing at the hip bone.

For most of us, however, a brisk, steady walking pace of three and a half miles an hour will move us along well and meet every prescription for conditioning and relaxation.

Starting Slow

It's not possible to get any really effective conditioning exercise without a striving, driving pressure that in the beginning usually causes some discomfort. By starting slow and working up to a fast pace we can minimize that.

For the first hundred yards, it seems better for me and I think for most of us simply to amble along at two or two and a half miles an hour, head down, shoulders relaxed and slouching, stomach sagging, just letting yourself go.

It takes more than a little forcing to move the shoulders back, the head back, the chin, the chest out, the stomach in, and above all to stride along and stride along rapidly. And it may take a few days, or a few weeks or even a few months, before the full reward comes through. But believe me, it does, and it comes through very fast, once it comes.

That is, within half a mile or a mile you feel a lift, an easy, smooth, relaxed gliding strength of walking. You really feel after the first mile that you can go on and on. And after two or three or four or five miles you feel just as well or even better.

Walking as an exercise is the easiest, most natural, most common way that we can keep our bodies from degenerating.

8 · When to Walk

WALKING THE FIVE MILES from my office to my home every evening is a big chunk out of my life. That hour a day represents about one-sixth or one-fifth of my waking hours when I'm not actually at work. I can tell you it's a marvelously well-spent hour. Of course if you walk to or from work, as I do, you can subtract the time you would have wasted sitting in a car or bus. And what a contrast with driving. Instead of building up tensions fighting the rush-hour traffic, you pass it as you stride along. This seems to me the perfect time to do my walking. Naturally, this will vary from person to person. Early risers often walk in their neighborhoods before they go to work.

Senatorial Walking

I also do a great deal of walking all day long. Here's what I do in the Senate. When the bell rings on the floor of the Senate for a roll-call vote, I'm usually in my office, which is in the New Senate Office Building, a third of a mile away. To get to the Capitol and the Senate floor from the New Senate Office Building I can take either of two routes. One is my good-weather route and the other is for bad weather, when I can't go outside without getting my gray flannel "toga" wet. In bad weather I go down three flights of stairs to the basement of the New Senate Office Building, walk through the basement of the Old Senate Office Building, through another long tunnel to the Capitol, and up three flights of stairs to the Senate Chamber. I vote and then return by the same route. In good weather, although the distance is about the same, the stairs are not quite as many. Two flights of stairs from my office, out the door of the New Senate Office Building, up First Street to Constitution Avenue, across Constitution Avenue and across the Capitol grounds, up the stairs on the Senate side of the Capitol and into the Senate Chamber. The round trip from my office to the Senate floor and back is at least the equivalent of two-thirds of a mile, especially with the energy required by two steps at a time on the up and down stair climbs.

Since I have been in the Senate I have answered more than four thousand roll calls. That means I've covered about nine hundred miles. On a typical day, depending on the number of roll calls and the number of times I have to go to the floor with or without roll calls, I get two or three miles of walking simply by moving from my office to the Senate floor.

Now this isn't the only way I could go. I could walk from my office to the other end of the Senate Office Building, take an elevator down to the basement, get on the little tram car that shuttles senators from the New and Old Senate Office Buildings to the Capitol, walk from the tram car to a little escalator, up the escalator to another elevator, and up in the elevator to the floor.

If I do not use the elevators or the tram car or the escalator, it takes me about six minutes to go from my office to the floor, 12 minutes round trip on foot. It takes four and a half to five minutes, depending on how long the wait is, if I use the moving vehicles. So I save one minute on a one-way trip and get virtually no useful exercise if I don't walk all the way.

Walking Senators

A number of other senators have discovered this. Senator Herman Talmadge of Georgia, for example, Senator

Harry Byrd of Virginia, Senator Abe Ribicoff of Connecticut, and Senator John Pastore of Rhode Island almost always walk from their offices to the Senate floor and back. Depending on where their offices are, and whether or not they take the stairs or elevators, if they cover the three miles in a day they use up 150–200 calories, tone up their muscles, relax their tensions, and waste virtually no time in the process.

You can do the same thing in your office, in your shop, in your store or in your home, by following the same prescription.

How far are you from the store? Few of us live more than a mile or so away. The problem, you say, is lugging home a huge bag of groceries or other things you buy. One way is to use a cart to trundle the goods home, another is to have the store deliver them. Another is to get double exercise credit by actually doing the job of carrying the packages home. If you are an eager beaver on this exercise kick and you're buying groceries for a big family, you might want to take three or four trips down to the store. Now that's crowding the hero's bench and I don't expect you to go that far, but do ask yourself, Is that trip in the automobile necessary? Wouldn't it be just as simple and almost as quick, especially with the inconvenience of parking, to walk and carry, instead of drive.

Climb Those Stairs

And consider the stair climb. If you work in a big building—on the sixth or seventh floor, say, or even the tenth or twelfth floor—it may seem idiotic to suggest that you walk up the stairway. Well, I'm suggesting exactly this. Dr. Paul Dudley White, the heart specialist who treated President Eisenhower and is recognized as one of the foremost specialists in the world, is in his seventies and he says he rarely passes up an opportunity to take the stairs instead of the elevator. Few things are better for your heart than stair climbing.

I can remember when medical advice was the opposite. In those days you gave your heart as little work as possible and never climbed stairs if you could avoid them. Modern medicine has found that this is the worst kind of advice. Climb those stairs! And, of course, if you work on the twentieth, thirtieth, or fortieth floor there is nothing to keep you from taking the elevator to the tenth floor and walking up, or walking up to the tenth floor and taking the elevator up. When you go out for lunch you may have a cafeteria right in your building or near the building. Try walking to one a mile or two away, have a light, quick lunch and walk back. You'll find that between the walk and the lightness of your lunch, it will not only help your waistline but brighten up your noonday and make you more alert and energetic for the rest of the afternoon.

Find a Special Time

If none of these suggestions seems workable, there is no reason why you can't make walking an end in itself. This may mean getting up half an hour earlier and walking in the neighborhood. Senator Fulbright likes to do that. He says he'd feel uncomfortable walking at a vigorous pace in his street clothes to the Senate Office Building but he finds it a pleasure to walk around his neighborhood in the morning. So does Senator John Pastore. You may say, Well, I can't afford the extra time; to take half an hour or an hour just to walk is too much time out of my life. Look at it this way, you won't have to sleep as much. Surprising as it sounds, I mean that. If you sleep one hour less than you sleep now, no matter how much that is, and walk for one hour instead, you will be a healthier person who will probably live longer and certainly feel far better. If you now rise at seven, get up at six. If you're a lark and feel wide-awake in the morning, this will be surprisingly easy. If you're an owl, there is another prescription for you. Take your walk at night, just before dinner, just after dinner, or just before you go to bed. You may miss some television time, you may have to skip that crossword puzzle you've been doing for years, you may miss that usual nightly snooze on the couch before you go up to bed, but make it a habit and you'll find it one of the most rewarding and pleasant ones you've ever developed.

Is Walking Safe?

One question that comes up in connection with evening walks is a product of our mid-twentieth-century life. Are the streets safe?

Who wants to increase his chances of being robbed, mugged or murdered?

You may have a point, but then again you may not. To reduce the chances of being robbed, a woman should *not* walk carrying a purse. Whether you're a man or a woman, don't dress as if you had any money.

If you are taking a walk from your house in the evening, there is no reason why you can't put on the most casual old clothes you can get—blue jeans, an old sweater, walking shorts. In the summer wear a tee shirt and walking shorts. You will look like an unlikely prospect for any holdup man. Once in a while we read about a psychopath who goes around shooting people simply for the perverse joy of it. Fortunately, these maniacs are very rare indeed. The overwhelming majority of assaults, except sexual attacks on women, are for the purpose of getting money. If you're casually dressed in sports clothes or old clothes, you just aren't a good prospect, and muggers are likely to pass you up.

Karate, Anyone?

If you're female, don't walk alone after dark in any neighborhood that you consider suspect. There are ways of protecting yourself if you're not absolutely sure. There are all kinds of equipment you can get, including shrill, loud whistles and very loud alarms that go off when dropped on the sidewalk. But the best precaution for a woman walking alone is a dog, preferably a big one. If you can get yourself a German shepherd, a Doberman pinscher, or any kind of big dog, a would-be attacker or rapist will give you a mighty wide berth. And of course walking a dog is not only a fine inspiration for establishing your habit of walking, it's a real favor to that dog. Nothing can make him happier.

There is one other prescription for safety that at first may sound far more spectacular than any you could consider seriously: learning karate for self-defense. On the basis of everything I've seen and heard, any potential rapist who attacks a woman karate expert will never have rape in his heart or mind again. A woman who is proficient at karate can disable the biggest professional athlete—primarily, of course, because of the surprise element. Such women feel completely secure, I'm told, under almost any circumstances.

In 1971 membership in karate schools was at a record 148,000. But if you intend to become a karate expert, be sure you have the time and determination to devote at least one solid year to learning it. The quickie ten-hour course in self-defense from your YWCA is more dangerous than helpful because it will give you false confidence. It takes a minimum of twelve to thirteen months to be able to protect yourself under most conditions, and that is after training pretty religiously all those months.

If you do stick with it, there can be a handsome pay-off. Take the case of Shirley Wells, of Denver, Colorado. Newspapers recently reported that when Shirley stopped her car to dislodge a box caught underneath it, a man approached her carrying a knife. He demanded that the five-foot-four, 110-pound young woman drive him where he wanted to go. Shirley snapped back with an elbow jab and two lightning kicks, one smashing the man in the chin. He fell to the ground, stabbing himself in the thigh on the way.

Shirley Wells just happens to hold a black belt in karate. That doesn't keep her from being pretty and attractive, but it certainly makes her free to walk anywhere she wishes, any time, without fear of rape. But remember that this woman is a karate black belt holder, which means that she has spent many, many months in training and discipline to develop her skill. It seems that nothing in this world that is worthwhile comes without effort, self-discipline, and time.

If you're a woman who doesn't find it practical to have a dog or to learn karate, then unfortunately, in many parts of our troubled country at the moment, you'll have to confine your walking, as well as your running or jogging, to the daylight hours.

This has really become a serious limitation in our American freedoms. We are losing the freedom to walk our streets at night.

The Right Schedule

You can walk not only early in the morning or in the dark in the evening, but you can walk in the broad, bright sunlight of noon, early afternoon, and late morning. So walk every day, and by walking every day I mean walk at least forty-five minutes to an hour a day, at one time, in one single stretch. Cover a full three or four miles without stopping, or at least stopping not more than a minute or so.

And be sure to get in those walks on week ends. It's strange, but some of the most faithful weekday walkers forget about week ends, which can be different and even more delightful. Week ends are the times when you can get out on the nature walks. You can walk the golf courses, trails through the woods, the country roads. Week ends are the times when you can take adventure walks as they do in Europe, walking from one town to another.

9 · Where to Walk

WHERE YOU WALK depends entirely on what you like. If you really want to, you can learn more about your community in a few weeks than almost anybody else in town knows. You can start off by walking two or three miles away from your house on the street that goes by your house. Then you can drive your car to another part of town and walk there. You're going to be astonished by what you find out about your town, even if it's a small one.

The People

Of course the first thing most of us notice is the people. And the wonderful thing about the people is that the overwhelming majority are friendly. If you smile and wave and say hello or good morning or have a nice day, people will smile, wave, say good morning, have a nice day back. And you will be brightening a moment, or in some cases the day, of the person you greet.

Sometimes in a big city you will get a blank stare. But even in big cities the response is far more often surprised or friendly. You'll find that people in different sections are really not very different in their friendliness. If they're working in the yard—mowing the lawn or tending flowers— and you make a comment about its attractiveness as you pass, they smile and respond warmly. Of course you can't make this an interview session unless that's what you want to do. Because if you do, you won't walk, you'll talk!

Just observe people's dress, their shape, their size, the way they move, and especially the different faces you see: young, old, lined, ugly, seamed, beautiful, tired, fresh, happy, sad, black, white.

One thing I've learned by looking at thousands of people over the years, in various parts of various cities, is that not many generalizations apply—no color, group, sex, or age has a corner on joy, exuberance, sadness, meanness.

But a few generalizations do apply. Most but not all people are pleasant, friendly, helpful if you want them to be, interested and responsive. It doesn't make any difference what part of town you go to or what kind of person you talk to. If you really do like people and they're more interesting to you than things, then the place for you to walk is in the city, in the crowded areas where the children play and where the people trudge back and forth to work or to the store.

You can see all kinds of people and enjoy them.

Nature Walks

If it's grass and trees and flowers that you like, then park your car in the suburbs and walk. Enjoy the great variety of architecture. The suburban areas of most of our cities have a wide array of different kinds of homes. And it's great to see how most people take deep pride in their homes, in the trimness of their lawns, and in the trees and shrubs they use to landscape their yards.

If you love the wide-open expanses of those almost endless greens of a golf course, look for one fairly near you. You are almost sure to find one handy unless you live in the heart of a big city. Golf-course walking can be a delight. Early in the morning it's all yours, and if it's a public course it's yours as much as any other taxpayer's any time of day. Golf courses are made for walking—a carpet of thick, springy, green, velvety grass under your feet and the fragrance of the grass—Wow!

If you've ever been a golfer it takes little imagination to

think of yourself hitting a 250-yard drive and a beautiful dead-to-the-flag approach, or chipping smartly out of the bunker as thousands applaud your victory over Jack Nicklaus. All in your Walter Mitty mind, of course.

Measuring your walking over a golf course is easy because the distance between the tee and green is specified at every tee. You know just how far you're walking. If you walk a typical eighteen-hole golf course tee to green, and add a little for green to tee distance, you'll cover about four miles. It can be a delightful hour's workout.

If there is no public course near where you live, don't give up. You probably won't be chased from a private course if you walk on it when it's not crowded and don't try to play on it.

Washington Walking

Few places offer the great attractions that Washington offers to a walker. But maybe I feel that way because I know Washington so well now. There's the unique towpath that runs from Georgetown mile after mile after mile along the banks of the Potomac. You don't have to worry about hills or rocks or climbing for at least ten miles of it, and very few want to walk that far. But even the rocky part is challenging and fun. The walk changes with each season and is always lovely. Although it was severely damaged by hurricane Agnes and the floods that collapsed the sides of the Barge Canal, this is still a charming, pleasant, and easy walk.

But far and away the most charming walk of all is one the National Park Service has made through much of Rock Creek Park, the Glover Archbold Nature Walk.

This is actually a series of breathtaking walks that vary from a quarter-mile to a mile, all sequential, so that you can walk about four miles in one direction and then four miles back. The trail takes you on the steep side of a ravine, along a creek heavily forested with majestic trees soaring more than a hundred feet into the air. You are covered with a canopy of green leaves in the spring, summer, and fall and of beautiful snow-draped branches in the winter.

This is a far more rugged walk than the walk up the towpath. Glover Archbold Nature Walk requires that you walk down a steep incline that gradually moderates, and then up and down along the path of a little creek and then up another climb, and the adventure is repeated in great variety throughout the walk.

Then there is the bicycle path along another section of the Potomac and Rock Creek Park. This is a pleasant and different kind of walk that takes you past the Lincoln Memorial and the Kennedy Center, then through a delightful section of Rock Creek Park. But it has two hazards. One is the whizzing bicycle riders who go past on both sides of the narrow path and ring you off it as they zip by. The second is the constant, fast-moving automobile traffic that zooms by you, coughing up the carbon monoxide as you walk. The towpath has its bicycles too, but they are far fewer and there are no automobiles. The Glover Archbold Nature Walk has no bicycles or automobiles. It's all yours.

Your Town Comes Alive

My own walk home every evening is not a scenic walk by any stretch of the imagination. The first few hundred yards are across the green Capitol grounds and then up Massachusetts Avenue, with stop lights every other block and heavy traffic everywhere.

But you can't find a walk anywhere that doesn't have some interest. This is true of my walk home. I walk up Massachusetts Avenue two and a half miles to Dupont Circle, then up Connecticut Avenue another two and a half miles to Ordway Street, and up Ordway Street to my house. Along Massachusetts Avenue the population for the first mile or so is largely black—friendly, outgoing people who wave, smile, say hello. Sometimes they ask me about their problems and I tell them we'll discuss their problems if they walk along with me. I walk by Seventh Street, a semi-skid row area peopled by black men and women, mostly men, sitting on benches and usually drinking out of bottles concealed in brown bags or stretched out on the grass sleeping it off. They're also friendly and often tease me or offer a drink.

Then comes the long block between Sixteenth and Seventeenth streets on Massachusetts that contains the Canadian Embassy, the Brookings Institution, the Australian Embassy, the Philippines Embassy. The population changes color from black to white, but the greetings continue. These greetings don't come automatically. They come because during the months and years I have walked up Massachusetts Avenue I have always said hello, smiled, waved. And people like to respond.

Then I pass Dupont Circle, where the long-haired kids hang out. I often hear drums or a guitar as I approach. Next there's a series of outdoor restaurants. By the time I walk by those restaurants I'm so hungry that the aroma of steak and chicken is very tantalizing indeed. Then it's up the long hill past the Washington Zoo, Ordway Street, and home. As walks go, this might be called dull and unattractive. But familiarity and awareness have turned it into a joy for me— changing, interesting, amusing, full of life. I'm sure that if you try, you can find a walk between where you work and where you live that's every bit as interesting as the walk I have from the Capitol to my home. If you don't think so, just try saying hello to people who pass by—smiling and waving. But if they insist on talking to you, tell them they have to walk along with you. When I say this people respond by saying, Well, I'll write you a note.

Work While You Walk

This section is for those who like to be fully occupied. You can work while you walk, but of course you have to pay the price. To my mind, the great joy and value of walking is that it enables you to relax completely, to be at one with nature and empty your mind of tensions and worries.

But you may not be so concerned with tensions and worries. You want the exercise, you want to get out, but you have work to do. Well, you can take it with you. You can take it with you in the first place simply by carrying a pencil and paper. How often do happy, useful ideas or even inspirations come to us and vanish from our memory when we get back to record them? That's happened to me so often that I always carry a pencil and paper to make reminder notes as I walk.

One time when I had a pencil but no paper, I used flat rocks to jot down my inspirations from on high. When I got home I found that the notes which had been penciled so clearly on the rocks had disappeared, vanished forever. I could neither decipher what was left nor recall a single great idea. Moral: Pencil *and* paper, or forget it and smell the flowers.

It may be that you want to work constantly while you walk, or at least more often than a notebook and paper would permit. In this case an investment may be worth your while.

I have found that a tape recorder is indispensable. I use it at home when I wake up at night, and I carry it in my briefcase for plane trips and hotel stopovers.

The small portable recorders are also very useful when you're walking. Simply flick on the switch and let the thoughts induced by exercise, the fragrance of the out-of-doors, a passing face, or a brief conversation be recorded for transcription at your convenience.

Relax While You Walk?

Yes, I agree it is a contradiction to talk about walking—striding at a rapid, three-and-a-half-mile-an-hour pace—and relaxing at the same time.

It's not nearly as hard as you may think. And I suspect the reason I can walk for several miles and feel energized, actually far more rested at the end of the walk than at the beginning, is because walking does enable you to let go of your tensions. Letting go is the principle, the name of the game, the very essence of relaxation.

And walking makes you do exactly this. Your intense concentration on other things diminishes. You shift gears from mental and emotional pressure to physical effort. And because you can't do everything at once, as you shift you subconsciously let go of mental and emotional tension. That relaxes and eases you and, I find, energizes you.

10 · Notes on Walking

IN MY HOME STATE of Wisconsin children have recently taken up walking for various charitable causes, asking merchants to donate a certain amount for each mile each child walks. This is one of the most inspired, delightful, and wholesome ideas to become popular in our country in a long time. It is happening in other areas besides Wisconsin now, but it has still received far too little notice. It combines what is good in health and what is good for the spirit.

Our children, with their wonderful idealism, are contributing something important by walking for a good cause. When they walk a grueling ten miles or even twenty miles or thirty miles because they believe in some charity, some cause, that really does something for the spirit. It is a contribution of the flesh, a painful, difficult, hard-earned, and healthy way to contribute.

Frankly, I was surprised that children who have been so pampered could walk the distances some of them do. But I've seen them walking in the rain in Fond du Lac, walking on scorching hot days in Milwaukee, walking through the snow in Madison, walking because they feel for hungry children in a foreign country or because they want to help some oppressed minority group.

It's a great idea, it's catching on, and anything we can do to make it catch on more will do a world of good for our children in mind and body and spirit.

Family Walk

When I was a boy of ten my eight-year-old sister, my twelve-year-old brother, my father and mother, and I took our one and only walk as a family. We had a dog then, a big Airedale whom we loved. We walked along the streets of Lake Forest, the lovely suburb of Chicago where we lived. We walked two or three miles to the cemetery and then along the lake. The dog threw a fit. I fought with my brother. My sister fell in a mud puddle with her new dress. We had such a marvelous time that we talked about it for years afterward. Why in the world our family never again took a walk together is beyond me. It was really a joy—to me, anyway.

Thirty years later, history repeated itself in a way. After I was elected to the Senate, my wife Ellen and I and our children—my son Ted and daughter Cici and her daughters, Mary Ellen and Jan Cathy—walked the five miles out to Ellen's parents' house one day. It was a funny, enjoyable walk full of all kinds of humorous incidents. Teddy played the delightful clown, as he always does, and the girls teased him. And yet that was the only walk we ever took as a family.

Maybe family walks aren't in the cards for me. Still, with a little effort and a little organization, I'm sure we could have had regular walks that would have been lots of fun for all of us, full of the give-and-take and humor and joy a family can bring each other when they do things together.

Now that I reflect on it, I think the reason we didn't take more family walks is that they would have been a forced thing. And in our free country probably the greatest source of tyranny is the autocratic family. This is something that has always gone against the grain with me. I hate to see a family in which the father or mother decides that something like walking together is a good thing and then starts cracking the whip like a drill sergeant, telling the brood to fall out and walk whether they like it or not.

I would rather lean over the other way. If your own example of walking daily is not contagious, if your husband or wife doesn't join you and the children don't want to go along—well, freedom is freedom. They may want to do their own thing and even develop self-discipline in their own way. The way to get the family to exercise right, eat right, relax sufficiently, in my view, just has to be by example.

Really See America

The most striking thing I have found in walking is the real beauty of this country. Walking is one way of seeing America literally at its grass roots. And this is an astonishingly delightful and beautiful country. Just this past year I've been walking on suburban and city streets not only in Washington but in Wisconsin and in other states.

I've never seen yards neater, trimmer, grass more carefully mowed or trimmed, flowers more profuse and abundant, houses so neatly painted, everything picked up and in order. And I've never seen more really beautiful homes. When you walk often and see the beauty of America, you see it intimately, you see it closely, at first hand, fingertip to fingertip and nose to nose. You smell it, you taste it, you savor it and get to love it in a way you cannot love it if you don't literally walk over it, walk around it, walk through it.

IV· RUNNING

11 · Persistence Is the Name of the Game

UNLESS YOU'RE ALREADY a distance runner, you should approach running or even jogging with the same caution as you would a hot stove or a rattlesnake.

You can't be too careful. Many a new enthusiast determined to find the quick way to bring himself into better condition has done himself more harm than good by approaching jogging or running too suddenly and without preparation.

The fact is that you can run five miles. You can run it easily and you can do this if you're twenty-five, thirty-five, forty-five, fifty-five, sixty-five, or, yes, seventy-five. You can feel better than you ever have in your life, you can have more stamina and endurance, you can strengthen your heart and probably lessen the chances of heart attack. You can greatly ease the tensions that prevent you from getting a good, healthy night's sleep. You can probably strengthen your ability to withstand arguments and to avoid headaches. You can do all these things, but you can't do them by going out tomorrow morning—probably not even three months from now—and running five miles.

Self-Discipline

The answer, as I say, is self-discipline. And you can be a far better athlete, stronger and in better shape than you were when you were twenty or twenty-five, unless you were a real whiz-bang at that age.

I speak as one of the worst athletes who ever put on a football uniform for Yale. No matter how inadequate you may be as a natural athlete, how little your natural physical endowments may have given you in the way of athletic capability, you can become a good long-distance runner if you have one quality, and that quality is persistence. I mean it when I say that when you become that long-distance runner you will find that you are stronger, have more stamina, than you had when you were in high school or college.

I'm sure that I can do more push-ups, that I can run farther, that I am less tired, that I have more stamina than I had thirty or forty years ago when I was earnestly striving for greater glory on the gridiron and in the boxing ring. But I had not learned the physical marvels that result when you go into real endurance training of the kind that comes from swimming long distances for twenty minutes or more a day, or running long distances twenty or thirty minutes or more a day.

Yes, you can do it. But as I say, approach it with the greatest caution.

Pace Yourself

In his autobiography Lincoln Steffens, the great muckraking journalist, tells about a nighttime ride he made as a boy to get a doctor for a woman who was very ill. When Steffens was only eight, before automobiles were invented, he was sent on his pony seven miles through the night into Sacramento. Just as he was about to leave he was given some invaluable advice that you can apply to your own approach to long-distance running. It was clear that little Steffens was eager to dash away on his pony and make that seven miles in a whooping sprint, but a wise man named Jim gave him this advice: "You start off easy, a gentle lope to, say, the main road. Then you walk the pony a hundred yards or so, then you lope again to about Dudens' place. By that time the pony will be warmed, but a bit winded. Walk again till he's easy, then go it; gallop a mile or so. Walk him again, fast, but walk; then you can run him a bit; not far. Trot half a mile—"

Then Jim asked, "How far can your pony run at full speed?" and Steffens told him a quarter of a mile.

"Well then, remember that," Jim said. "He can run only a quarter of a mile, and you have seven miles to go."

Steffens wrote, "By this time I was so dashed, so unheroic, that Jim may have seen my depression. He gave me a boost back up to the poetic. 'Now go,' he said; 'you are going to find out that the hero business is hard work, requiring judgment and self-control, not merely whip and spurs. And,' he added, 'your friend Mrs. Neely needs you tonight, you and a doctor. Good luck to you.'"

Jim's advice to young Lincoln Steffens is exactly the kind of advice we should give ourselves in starting to run long distance. Self-discipline and self-control; to restrain the temptation to do more than is good for you is absolutely essential.

Gradual Build-up

Your build-up must be gradual. And this is why that discipline is so vital: *You must stay with your program of first walking and then running short distances at an easy pace every single day without a miss. You must do it in rain, or dry weather, in snow, on ice, in winter, in summer, in fall, in spring—you must do it when you've had three or four hours of sleep, and sometimes you'll have to cut your sleep short by an hour in order to do it. But do it—never, ever miss a day.*

For everyone who would achieve the benefits of long-distance running there must be a hundred who gave it up after two or three days or two or three weeks or two or three months.

But that self-discipline can be far more than a game because it strengthens your self-control in every other phase of your life, and self-discipline is the secret of freedom.

Before you go out to walk or run, make sure you have the right kind of clothes on. Usually people already own the right kind of clothes. Just make sure your shoes are comfortable. Tennis shoes are fine, and any old, easy shoes—for example, Hush Puppies or something similar—are appropriate. Almost any easy, comfortable, relaxed clothes in which you feel natural are completely appropriate for running.

To build up running you should start walking. Walk a good, fast, striding pace. Then trot slowly and I mean slowly, taking it very easy, for a block. Walk a block, run a block; keep an eye on your watch, make sure you know what time you started. And when you've been out for about fifteen minutes, turn around and start back. Walk a block, run very slowly a block, walk a block, lope very slowly a block, and get back to the house. If you want to do it, there's no reason why you can't follow this routine on your way to work, on your way to shop or pick up the children, at noon when you go out to lunch, or any other time.

Exercise Nut

Now I know the principal thing likely to inhibit that little one-block-at-a-time jogging is that you may expect people who see you to think it looks peculiar. Well, a few of them may but most of them won't. I've been doing this for years, and I'm an expert on people looking at you and thinking you look peculiar. After all, I'm fifty-seven years old, I'm a United States Senator, and you don't exactly expect to see a fifty-seven-year-old senator running down the street. I mean it when I say that the ridicule has been infinitesimal, that for everyone who thinks you're a little nuts, there are ten who will admire your effort to get somewhere in a slight hurry or to get yourself in good physical condition.

For two weeks just keep up your walk-a-block, jog-very-slowly-a-block. During that two weeks get an appointment with your doctor and have him give you a thorough examination, especially of your heart, to be sure that you are in good physical condition. Tell him exactly what you are doing and follow his advice to the letter. And after two weeks, see if you can go just a little farther and I mean just a little. Not much. I know if you press yourself you can go a great deal farther, but see if you can go just a little farther in the same time. This will mean that you have to walk a little faster and run a little faster—not much, just a little. For the next two weeks go one extra block in the same half-hour. And after this second two weeks, I have a surprise in store for you. Go the same distance, but run two blocks and walk one block. Notice the time. You will be astonished at the way you are able to cover more distance in less time without walking or running any faster but simply running a little more than you walked.

Self-Restraint

The trick now is to restrain yourself from pushing ahead too fast. Stay with a one-block-walk, two-block-easy-run for at least another month, then have your doctor give you one more checkup with emphasis on your heart. If he says everything is A-OK, you can start off on the second phase. On this you can run the full half-hour but it should be at a very slow, easy pace and as soon as it becomes significantly uncomfortable—as soon as you have to breathe a little harder or your knees feel a little weak—resume your walk. Stay with that half-hour run—it can be a twenty-five-minute run or a thirty-five-minute run or a forty-minute run, espe-

cially if you have that much distance to cover to your office
or to the store—until you find you can do it easily. This may
take a couple of months; it may take three or four. At this
point you should have another physical exam and then begin
to push yourself a little harder. Not much. Don't sprint.

Keep at it, slowly, surely, relentlessly, until you're just
about ready to go the five miles and to do it in forty-five or
maybe forty minutes. By now, whether you are twenty-five,
thirty-five, forty-five, fifty-five, sixty-five, seventy-five, you
are a trained athlete and literally in better physical condition than 90 percent of the football players who play in the
National Football League. You can run farther and in better
time than most college athletes. You will find that you sleep
much better and don't need as much sleep, that your nerves
are steadier, that you're happier, easier to get along with,
more relaxed, that you can control your weight much better.
But to achieve all these things and keep them you must stay
with it. If you start running six days a week and then three
and then two and skipping a week or two weeks, pretty soon
you're the same old sluggish person you were before.

Every Day All Over Again

Physical condition is something you have to re-
achieve every single day of your life. As in sensible dieting,
you can't crash yourself to success. To be sure you are in
good shape, the secret is not to get in good shape, it is to *stay*
in shape. And to do that you have to be willing to stay with
this all the days of your life. There are days when it's good
and days when it's bad. Days when you would rather run
than almost anything—when the air smells good and the sky
is clear and the sun is bright, the breeze is cool, people say
cheery, happy hellos and you smile and wave at them with
joy in your heart. And there are many, many days when you
dread running, when you want to quit after that first half-
mile, when it's cold and rainy, when you've had too little

sleep and there are many other things that you would like to do or should be doing. But day-to-day persistence is the answer.

Now let me tell you immediately that I am almost unique in making this argument. Dr. Kenneth Cooper, who is probably the outstanding authority in the country on conditioning through running, contends that careful studies show that four or even three days a week of running are enough to stay in condition.

Of course Dr. Cooper is physiologically correct. The reason I argue for seven days is that I don't know anybody who has the self-discipline and the will to keep running three days a week. If you make an excuse for one day, it's too easy to make an excuse for two or three or four. The weather, your physical condition, the demands of your business or your family will always combine with that built-in human inertia which all of us have to keep you from going ahead. And once you miss a week and only work out for one day or two days, you are in real trouble, because the week-end athlete, especially the person who runs and who tries to make up by running full steam one or two days a week, is the one who puts his heart in the most jeopardy.

Your system will adjust to that daily workout just as it adjusts to the three meals a day or four meals a day that you eat. It is most important to you to run every day as part of your routine; this makes it easier because it's automatic, as automatic as brushing your teeth, going to bed at night, or having dinner.

Fallout Benefits

Just consider the fallout benefits. If you run to work and back, you immediately and directly save money on transportation by bus, taxi, or automobile. If you enjoy eating, that five-mile run will enable you to eat another 500 or 600 calories a day without gaining an ounce, or if you like to lose, you can maintain your present diet and lose about a pound a week. That five miles of running means that you burn up 3,500 calories a week, and it just happens that 3,500 calories equals one pound. Then there's the advantage of looking better, and you're bound to look better. It will show in the clearness of your skin, in the clearness of your eyes, in your serenity and relaxation, in the inches that will melt off your waist, in the strength that will come to your arms and legs.

Dr. Cooper has told me that tests have shown again and again that people who run two or three or four or five miles always turn out to be physically stronger, that running has actually given them the kind of strength that others lack.

And you lengthen the odds that you'll live longer, for running opens up additional blood vessels. Most studies indicate that those who have developed this persistent athletic capacity are far more likely to survive a heart attack. If you stay with this moderate build-up every single day, so your system becomes accustomed to it, you are giving your heart and your whole cardiovascular system the best kind of daily tonic it can possibly have, which is regular, moderate, physical exercise of the same kind, the same dimension day after day.

It is the precise opposite of the week-end crash athlete who goes all out in competitive sport every other Sunday or even every week end, putting his heart under great tension and stress.

At Sixty-five—Better Shape than Staubach or Bench

From the standpoint of heart and circulation, the sixty-five-year-old woman who walks five or six miles a day, provided she walks it continuously, is in better physical condition than Johnny Bench or Roger Staubach. The human body has become marvelously adapted for action. But in the last couple of generations we have let it sag into disuse, and the degenerative diseases, particularly heart disease, is the price we are paying for that. The answer is to gradually, gently, slowly work your body back into shape and then keep at it; once you do, you find that this remarkably tough, strong body can serve your mind, your disposition, your spirit as never before.

Who says that youth is the best time of life—the period of teens and early twenties? Why do they say that? They say that primarily because physically our strength and health, our stamina, our capacity for enthusiasm, or just plain *joie de vivre* happens to be at its peak in the teens and early twenties.

This is probably so for most of us. But only because we are so terribly neglectful of endurance training. We certainly need not be so.

Can running actually improve our youthful vitality? It can indeed, but it can do it much better if we pay attention to a few other things, like diet and relaxation of body and mind.

12 · Running for Profit and Pleasure

IT'S STRANGE what interests people about running. But the most commonly asked question by people who wonder about my running to work is a practical and simple one that may be inhibiting you from running to work too.

They ask, "Senator, if you run five miles to work, you must come in sweating and perspiring with a fragrance that might do great glory to a gym. It must be something else in an office."

Or they say, "Senator, you run to work in casual sport clothes. Can you work as a senator all day and go on the floor of the Senate and into those august committee rooms dressed like someone bumming around the house or yard?"

The answer to those questions is very easy for me. When I streak across the Capitol grounds, over C Street and into the New Senate Office Building, I go straight to the New Senate Office Building gym, where I have a locker. I strip, take a refreshing cold shower, rub myself down with towels, weigh myself on the scale, proceed to put on my senatorial clothes, and come up smelling like a rose.

Other senators have had to dress at home, get into their cars, and sit through half an hour or more of traffic. They just can't feel nearly as clean and neat and fresh as I do.

How About You?

Now you may ask, Well, Senator, that's fine for you but how about me? I don't have a locker room in my office. I don't have a shower, I don't have the facilities for washing and rinsing.

Well now, just a minute. Maybe you have all those things and don't know it. For a couple of years before I discovered the locker room in the New Senate Office Building, I used to do all those things in my bathroom. All you really need is access to the privacy of a bathroom for a few minutes while you strip, sponge bathe, and change. And if you're careful to get to the office a little early you can probably use the office bathroom facilities without infuriating your fellow workers.

There must be some place in your office where you can hang your clothes. Once a week or so you'll have to bring fresh office clothes in and take your laundry home. But that's a small price.

Then at night you simply duck back into your bathroom, put your casual clothes on again, and are all set for the journey home.

I wouldn't be surprised if this simple absence of facilities is what stops many thousands of people who otherwise might very well run to work.

I can remember the late Senator Richard Neuberger of Oregon saying that he would like to walk the three miles a day from where he lived but he was sure he would look and give off the fragrance of a refugee from Product X deodorant on television. He felt it would not only be demeaning and undignified but a good way to lose votes both on the Senate floor and from his visiting Oregon constituents. The answer to all this is a little ingenuity. I'm sure many Americans will overcome this sensitivity which years of television commercials have given us. Put on those casual clothes in the morning, walk or run to work, strip, shower or sponge off when you get to work, change into office attire, and reverse the process on the way home at night.

Look Silly

There are many alibis for not running and one of them is that it just looks silly for most people to go out and run. If you are a housewife or a businessman or a blue-collar worker or even a teenager and go running down the street, you may feel that neighbors or strangers will think you are a real odd-ball.

I recall that on a September morning as I was running down Massachusetts Avenue toward the Capitol, my running shorts showing bare legs and bony knees, not exactly what you would expect of a man of fifty-plus, a construction worker shouted at me, "Hey, you skinny old man, put some clothes on!"

But then there was the thoughtful and gracious lady who used to ride by me on the bus every morning and see me pounding away on the pavement as the bus rode by. She sent me a dozen roses with a note saying, "Keep it up, Senator. You look great!"

At least half of the dozens of bus drivers who drive by me wave and smile. Many cab drivers do too. There is a former cavalry colonel who stopped me one day to give me a book he had written about his cavalry unit in World War II. For many months he would flash by me and roll down his window and shout, "Atta boy, Senator!"

In the first chapter I talked about how we are all imprisoned in cages of health-destroying physical habits, and how this book presents some keys to help break out of them. One key is getting out and running and jogging, and I think a principal obstacle to its use is the fear that somebody is going to laugh at you.

The answer, of course, is that root cliché, SO WHAT! Let them laugh all the way to the graveyard!

13 · You Can't Run Away from Your Job

ONE BRIGHT, sunny, humid June morning, when I was running down Connecticut Avenue—just making the traffic light—a police car coming from the opposite direction passed me. As it passed, the policeman driving the car eyed me with a frown, as if he felt that I might have jumped the light. I ran on for another half-mile and barely made another traffic light. The same police car passed me going in my direction. A quarter-mile ahead it swung in front of me, moved over the sidewalk into an alley, and blocked my path. I was prepared to laughingly ask the policeman if he was going to arrest me for speeding, and if that didn't go over, to commend him for his alertness and his willingness to stop even running pedestrians if he thought a law had been violated.

After all, law and order is law and order and violations are violations—whether it's a traffic light or a tax report, a senator is not above the law. These thoughts went through my mind as the policeman looked up and said, "Well, Senator, what are you going to do about our pay bill?" The officer wasn't interested in any local pedestrian ordinance. He wanted more money, and in the District of Columbia that has to come from Congress.

I said, "Officer, the pay bill provides a 17-percent increase for you fellows and I'd thought you'd like it."

"Yeah, but how about retroactivity? It only begins on July 1 and this is June 16. It ought to be retroactive till"— and I interjected, "January 1."

He said, "That's right and that's not all. How about the educational benefits and the additional sick pay?"

I said, "Officer"—meanwhile running in place up and down, because I wanted to be sure that I got the full aerobic effect of this exercise in spite of the officer's intention to improve his lot—"I'd like to help you. I'm on the Appropriations Committee but I don't think I'm on the right subcommittee."

As it turned out, I wasn't on the right committee. The committee that handled the pay increase was not the Appropriations Committee. But I didn't realize that until I'd run another half-mile and the officer was far behind me.

"You fellows do a great job," I told the officer. "I'd like to do all we can to help. Let me look into it."

The officer started to lobby a little more and I gently jogged away with what I thought was a friendly smile. He didn't respond. His lips were turned down. He was still determined to get a commitment from me on the pay increase, and I felt that if he had been voting in Wisconsin, it was one vote I had lost.

As I ran across Calvert Street, headed for the bridge, I began to wonder why I hadn't just told that policeman he ought to get down on his knees and thank the good Lord he had a 17-percent pay increase that was almost three times the 5½-percent wage guideline in effect for the country as a whole. What kind of example is this to the country in stopping inflation if the federal government as an employer is this extravagant? By that time I was beginning to hit an uphill incline, just over the Taft Bridge on Connecticut. And all I could think of was Vince Lombardi's observation that fatigue makes cowards of us all, and I began to think of the velvety waters of the Hilton pool which would envelop me with another kind of exhaustion.

Clashing with the Pentagon

It's about 7:10 in the morning. I shut the front door, run to the street, cross the street to the sidewalk and go down the sidewalk on the way to the office.

The first couple of hundred yards are always easy: flat, then downhill.

That's the time when I think of what's going on that day— a hearing with the highly controversial Roy Ash, head of the powerful Office of Management and Budget. Ash is not only right at the hurricane's eye in the bitter battle between the Congress and President Nixon over priorities. He has been the chief executive officer of a huge conglomerate handling billions of dollars of defense contracts. How to handle Ash on priorities and Ash on conflict of interest raises a complex problem of timing and emphasis.

This is going to be an important day. All the television networks will be there, the *New York Times,* the *Washington Post,* the Associated Press, the United Press, the *Wall Street Journal,* and a variety of defense specialists and other press men, plus a big audience of correspondents from foreign countries, graduate students, staff people from Defense, the Department of State, and AID, as well as tourists, dropping in to see what a hearing in Washington is really like.

I am thinking, as I run down Ordway Street toward Connecticut Avenue, of asking Ash how he can reconcile the Administration's softness on military waste with its toughness on funds for fighting poverty.

Just as I formulate the question in my mind, a mail truck roars by and the driver leans out and says, "Hi, Senator." Roy Ash slips away and up comes the stop light at Ordway and Connecticut. It's still green but it's about to go amber, so I have to step up my eight-mile-an-hour pace to a sprint to make it across the street.

I run past the bread truck unloading at the Safeway store and on across Macomb Street and that little uphill incline by the Washington Zoo. Only long-distance runners really appreciate what it means to run up a hill. It really makes a difference. It's harder. You begin to breathe more. Thoughts about Budget Director Ash fade further away and you notice the fatigue beginning in your legs. That uphill incline of about a hundred yards is in the second half-mile and that second half-mile is the most difficult and painful segment of my five-mile run. Psychologically it's bad because it is just the beginning. There are almost five miles ahead. You already feel tired, you want to quit and walk. It's uphill, breathing isn't easy. But you stay with it and then comes a long downhill run. The light at Cathedral and Connecticut is just turning green. If you sprint, you can make it.

Golf-Course Running

I'll never forget the beauty of running over the Walt Disney World golf course at Orlando, Florida, in August of 1972, as the sun was coming up over the Florida palm trees. I bounced yard by yard, mile by mile over the verdant, springy carpet of fairway. And what a fairway! A special lawn mower keeps the grass tightly cut, and it's a particular kind of grass whose blades grow so close together that it's like one continuous weave. The discomfort evaporates, the labors of breathing are forgotten, as you run through the beauties of the morning and enjoy that moist, green, fresh, clean smell of grass. And I had acre after acre all to myself because nobody plays golf at this hour of the morning, especially at Disney World.

A few days later I was on the Onwentsia Country Club golf course in Lake Forest, Illinois, where I played hundreds of rounds in my college days. This too was an exquisitely manicured course. But it had been inundated with the heaviest rains in years: water standing in fairways, water in the bunkers.

For three happy mornings I would start on the first hole and run each of the eighteen holes, the distance between the green and tee. By running back and forth across the fairway and around the greens, I ran about five miles. The first morning I ran, my shoes and socks were soaked, so the next two mornings I ran barefoot. And what a delightful experience! Some of the great cross-country runners of the sixties used to run barefoot. When you run on a golf course there are virtually no problems. Even a lightweight shoe represents extra weight that you normally have to carry when you run, and when your foot has barefoot lightness, it's a joy that most of us haven't tasted since childhood. I ran mile after mile with my feet caressed by that cool, green, wonderful grass. Grass in the rough is thick but long. Grass on the fairway is short, and so thick and so flexible that running is more of a pleasure than ever. The discomfort of the abrasive rub of shoe against skin, the confinement of your feet in shoes, has all disappeared.

Run Over Childhood Memories

Why don't you try running in the places you played when you were a child? Go home, as I did, and try running down the sidewalks you used to enjoy when you were twenty, thirty, forty years younger.

Run along the river, the beach, even by the hospital where you were born, the home where you grew up, the school that gave you happy memories. Something happens to our past. All the dreams and problems dissolve. Only the happy good times remain in our memory. You'll find it that way when you revisit the places of your childhood and walk vigorously or jog or run where you used to play as a child. Try it.

V· SWIMMING AND OTHER SPORTS

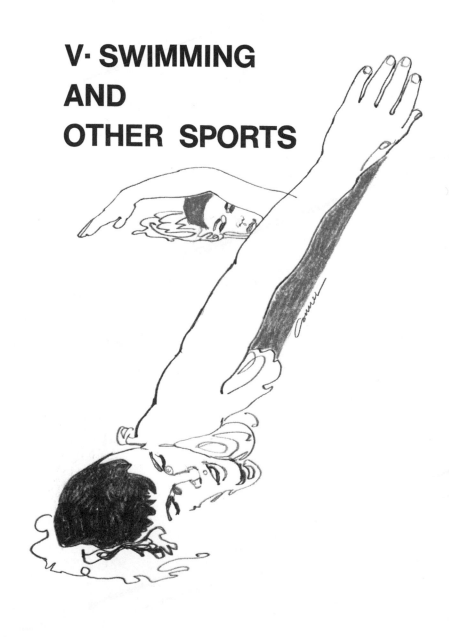

14 · Swimming

THERE ARE FEW if any human activities that conjure up happier visions than swimming. Most of us have fond memories of the beach or the old swimmin' hole. Or when we want to envision the good life at its epicurean best many of us think of the beautiful country-club pool, the kind you see in the movies or on television shows featuring fabulously wealthy people at play, including two or three abundantly endowed, bikini-clad young ladies reclining on the edge of the inviting cool blue water.

Swimming just has to be a delightful physical experience—voluptuous and invigorating. But it can also be an extraordinary test of endurance. I recall as a little boy reading about Gertrude Ederle, the indomitable, incredibly powerful woman who swam the English Channel in sixteen hours, swimming against the tide in those icy waters hour after grueling hour.

For most people to swim at Gertrude Ederle's pace for one minute would be a strain, but Miss Ederle kept on—a real triumph for the human will and spirit—all those hours to reach her goal.

To me that Ederle swim ranked with Lindbergh's flight to Paris. Both were astonishing achievements.

Today we have become softer and more physically degenerated than mankind ever has in history. The irony of it is that modern athletes are in the best condition in human history. Anyone who questions this has only to look at the phenomenal records of the distance runners. In recent years there has been an epidemic of better-than-four-minute miles —a time considered impossible for this distance thirty years ago. Even more astonishing is the tremendous record of swimmers and the times they are making in sprints and especially in distances. The records today's swimmers set are the result of their astounding endurance training.

Talk about triumph of the will and human purpose! It is one thing to swim the English Channel in one brilliant burst of effort, even though it could take ten or twenty hours. It's something else to go out every day and swim three or four hours a day, month after month, for years. This is just what our young people have done in building the strongest, healthiest, best-conditioned bodies the world has ever seen.

Does Swimming Turn You On?

Walking may bore or annoy you. If so, swimming can be your thing. If you swim steadily and vigorously, without letup, for twenty minutes or more every day, you will work your heart and circulatory system into good shape. You will enjoy the same health benefits you get from vigorous running for the same length of time or from an hour or so of rapid walking a day.

Most of us think of swimming as splashing in the water, diving in, coming out, playing, and just having a cooling, exhilarating ball without the grueling effort of swimming lap after lap. Some mean lolling around the pool or on the beach an hour for every minute they spend in the water.

That won't do. To obtain any real conditioning from swimming you must swim at a steady, rapid pace for twenty minutes or more.

When I was thirteen my father bought a summer place for our family in Canada. It was on the North Channel that connects Lake Superior and Lake Huron. That was before water skiing became popular, though we did a lot of aqua planing—that is, we'd get on a small board behind a power boat and have a great time zipping over the water. But the water was very cold, 55 or 60 degrees most of the time, so we spent only a little time in the water and lots of time in boats or sitting on docks enjoying the sun. From the standpoint of conditioning that kind of swimming is just useless.

Endurance Swimming Rare

Even when the water is ideal in temperature and convenience, I'm convinced that not one person in a hundred really swims in a way that will provide any conditioning benefit.

Just drop by a country-club pool or a pool around a luxurious hotel. You'll find the overwhelming majority of people lying on the side of the pool or on cushions or cots absorbing the sun. Once in a while they will drop into the water to cool off, swim a few strokes, float around, hang onto the side of the pool, and come out.

Back in the thirties, when I was a student at Yale, we had the finest swimming teams in the country. During that whole decade Yale was undefeated in any kind of dual meet. Our swimmers were among the best in the world and held many world records. But for anybody to swim three hours a day then would have been considered a rare fanaticism.

Today swimmers' training has undergone a stunning change. In Australia the great distance runners who gradually broke through the four-minute-mile barrier trained longer hours than runners had ever trained before. Trainers found that the body could stand a great deal more conditioning and training than had been thought possible. This knowledge was soon applied to swimmers. Now it's routine with any kind of first-class collegiate swimming team for the swimmers to actually swim vigorously for three or four hours daily.

The results have been astonishing. World records that

were thought to be impregnable have been broken easily. That very rare creature the long-distance runner or long-distance swimmer is undoubtedly in the best physical condition, in terms of heart and circulatory system, that man has ever enjoyed.

Twenty Minutes Will Do It

Few of us have three or four hours a day that we can devote to running or swimming, but twenty minutes every day, seven days a week, will bring you reasonably close to the level of conditioning, as far as your heart and lungs are concerned, that three hours will. It's very important, however, that those twenty minutes be consecutive and that they be concentrated and vigorous. If you're an average swimmer you might work toward achieving a distance of, say, nine hundred yards a day in eighteen minutes.

This is what I do just about every day between May 1 and November 1 in the pool at the Washington Hilton, which fortunately for me is just about halfway between my home and the Capitol. I get up at 5:45 A.M. to have plenty of time to do half an hour of calisthenics and then run from my house to the Hilton, getting there before 7:00 A.M. After changing into my trunks, I swim the thirty-six lengths that constitute nine hundred yards in that twenty-five-yard pool. Usually I then run the remaining three miles to the Capitol. However, sometimes in the heat of the summer my Achilles tendon gets painful and it's impossible for me to do the running. When that happens I walk from my house to the pool, swim the half-mile, and then walk to the Capitol. That vigorous swimming is an excellent substitute for running and gives me very close to the equivalent conditioning.

Mind and Spirit at Rest

Swimming is a marvelous change of pace from running. To move along at a steady pace isn't easy, and there's occasional discomfort and weariness involved, but there are few things like swimming for relaxing your mind and spirit. The velvety smoothness of the water, the refreshing coolness after a hard run, somehow push frustrations and emotional turmoil into the background and give you the closest thing to conscious and complete mental relaxation that you can achieve when you're physically active.

Gradual Build-up

As in running, it's a serious mistake in swimming to start off too vigorously. Very few people who haven't been swimming a great deal, even if they are good swimmers, are able to swim a half-mile right off the bat at a good pace. You build up to it the same way you build up to your running. Try swimming a good vigorous crawl until you feel uncomfortable or winded, then float on your back, side stroke or breast stroke or just rest at the end of the pool until you feel recovered. Any of these ways of resting is the equivalent of walking part of the distance as you work up into long-distance running.

I suggest that you start off by swimming a length at a good pace, then swim back using whatever is the easiest stroke for you—breast stroke, side stroke, or an easy back stroke in which you move by flipping your hands, which I feel is the most relaxed and easy method of keeping afloat and moving in the water. Then swim another reasonably vigorous crawl for one length and come back again floating easily along.

The first day, instead of swimming thirty-six lengths you may find that you swim twelve or fifteen in your allotted twenty minutes. After a week of this, try swimming two lengths with a fast crawl stroke, then taking one length the easy relaxed way, and then two fast lengths again.

A week later try swimming up and back three times, that is, six lengths, in a steady crawl stroke before you relax into your slower and easier swim pace. Continue to increase the amount of vigorous swimming, taking at least a month or six weeks to work into the half-mile swim at a steady crawl pace, and by the end of a season you'll find swimming that half-mile is something you can really look forward to.

The Complete Exercise

In many ways swimming is just about the best exercise there is. I prefer running because for me running is a whole lot more convenient. But swimming brings almost every muscle in the body into play and provides a far better toning-up method for the upper body, especially the arms and chest, than running does. Swimming strengthens and develops and challenges muscles that are not developed in modern life. Stomach muscles, back muscles, leg muscles, arms, chest, neck, you name it—swimming will bring them into play.

And it's a great kind of exercise to have in your exercise arsenal in case there's a period when you can't run because of some difficulty with your legs or feet.

Keep at It

Once again let me stress, however, that if swimming is going to be your conditioner you must do it every single day without exception. Every day. No matter what kind of iron will power you think you can develop, if you don't do it every day you'll find reasons for not doing it as often as you should and you'll begin to skip more and more days.

By far the best time to swim is when a pool first opens in the morning. Do your best to find a pool that opens early. At seven o'clock in the morning you can often get a pool all to yourself. This means you can swim without getting in anybody else's way and without having anybody get in yours. Of course swimming may be simply impossible for you if you don't have a swimming pool. You may say, How can I afford a swimming pool? A good question.

It's easy to afford a chance to run or walk. Anybody can do this without any expenditure at all, but how many people can buy a swimming pool? Well, not many. I can't afford one myself, but increasingly hundreds of thousands of Americans have built pools in their own yards, and millions have access to pools if they'll look around. If you belong to a club, that's one way of doing it. If you don't, there are public pools available in almost every city, including little towns in Wisconsin with 3,500 or 4,000 in population.

Look around your town or neighborhood and you'll be surprised how conveniently close a pool may be. And if you inquire about the hours when the pool is open, you'll probably find that early in the morning, or perhaps in the evening, you can have the pool pretty much to yourself.

Public Pools the Best

Often the best pools are not the private pools, because very few people can afford to build a large private pool. Public pools are usually bigger and more satisfactory for endurance swimming, the quality of the water is always maintained so that it's completely safe and sanitary, and the size is enough so that you can get a good workout by swimming lengths.

Many private pools are like the senators' pool in the Old Senate Office Building in the Senate. That pool is only thirty-four feet long, and in order to swim half a mile I have to swim about eighty lengths. Most of the swimming in a pool that small simply consists of pushing off one end and, after just a few strokes, finding yourself at the other. The actual swimming is so limited that the pool is not nearly as good a conditioner as the seventy-five-foot pool that is a fairly standard-size public pool.

If you swim at a country-club pool or a public one it's not

easy to persuade the authorities to get it the temperature that you enjoy. It makes a difference to me to have the water warm enough so that I don't shiver when I get into the pool. The water in the pool in the Old Senate Office Building is far too cold, and I come out a shade of purple and blue and shiver through the next hour or so. On the other hand, after a few weeks of the hottest days in July, the water at the Hilton pool in Washington is in the 80s, and it's enervating to swim nine hundred yards in a hot bath. If it's between the two, I'd take the warm water any time, but the ideal temperature is somewhere in the middle 70s, and with a little persuasion you can usually talk the authorities into maintaining that temperature. Most people seem to find it just what they want.

You're Alone

One of the distinct liabilities of the kind of exercise I'm talking about now—that is, swimming lengths, endurance swimming for twenty minutes or more without stopping—is that it is strictly a solo operation, solo in every sense of the word. Swimming for conditioning is anything but a social exercise. You can run with your friends, you can walk with your friends, but if you swim any distance, your friends may be there and you may be conscious of it but communication is just about impossible.

With all the swimming I've done for conditioning over the past five or six years, the only friend I can recall swimming with me is Chuck Percy, the extraordinarily well-conditioned Senator from Illinois. Chuck is an excellent athlete in superlative condition. He was a swimmer in college and is a far better swimmer than I am. He also has the kind of stamina and conditioning that enable him to keep swimming lap after lap. He went into the water at the same time I did and somehow I'm so competitive that I felt I had to keep up with him. But my communication was strictly one of competition, not the happy, give-and-take communication you can have with a good friend when you are walking or running.

This is both the great asset of long-distance swimming for conditioning and its shortcoming. Swimming is a great way to get away from it all. Nobody can stop you and ask for an autograph when you are swimming in a pool. Nobody's going to talk to you about what's wrong with the welfare-reform proposal or the foreign-aid bill or the imminent explosion in the Middle East.

That kind of interruption happens to me when I'm running or walking and it will happen to you in some other way in your neighborhood or wherever people know you if you run or walk. People can't understand why you can't stop for a conversation. When you're swimming, however, that's impossible. You not only can't talk with people, you can't see or hear them—there are no distractions.

Yes indeed, it can be boring but it can also be the right formula for a repetitive, pleasant relaxation that enables you to concentrate on your swimming, on the physical effort, and relax and let go of all your emotions and frustrations and (as we point out in another section) permit a shift in your brain waves into Alpha—that is, let go of those intruding thoughts that provoke and bother you and simply relax into pleasant and easy meditation. That's what I find is the joy of swimming.

15 · Baseball and Football Are for Softies

IT'S IRONIC that our country has never been more richly able to enjoy exercise and sports than we are now. Never has so much money been spent on sports. Never have so many people engaged in sports. And yet we are probably in the worst physical condition that mankind has ever suffered. People in this country are in worse condition than in many other countries simply because we work physically so much less than the people of other countries.

The sports activities that people engage in are fun or they wouldn't engage in them. They provide joy and pleasure but they don't increase longevity, and they don't provide any improvement in the circulatory system or build a strong heart.

In this chapter let's sit back and take a look at some of the most popular sports in America and consider what they might be able to do for the circulatory system.

First let's take a look at those that do little or nothing to condition the body, then we'll finish up with those that can do a great deal.

Fishing and Hunting

All the statistics show that two of the most popular sports in this country are fishing and hunting. Judging by the number of fishing licenses issued and the amount of money spent on fishing equipment, including outboards and boats and so forth, Americans are enthusiastic about fishing as a sport. And though it's a pleasant sport, I think very few would argue that fishing—even deep-sea fishing—provides the kind of exercise that anyone could call a conditioner. Conceivably fishing for deep-sea fish off the Gulf Coast, when you get a large tarpon on the line and struggle with him for an hour or two, could rate with any kind of long-distance running or swimming. But this isn't what most sport fishermen are talking about. They are talking about dropping a line into a nearby river or lake or creek, or about casting for trout or trolling over the back of a motor boat. This kind of activity may build patience, may provide the absence of distraction that permits meditation, and may offer the joy of the great outdoors, but *exercise* it is not.

To the extent that hunting requires long-distance walking, it can conceivably be good exercise, but it is usually interrupted by long periods of sitting and waiting. Inactivity is far more characteristic of hunting and fishing than activity. While fishing, the typical fisherman sits absolutely still, motionless, no muscles and action, no challenge to the heart. He might as well be at home watching television as far as exercise is concerned. The duck hunter sits in his blind; the man hunting deer may walk a few hundred yards or even half a mile or so from his car to get into the brush where the deer is, but then he sits as quietly as he can, waiting for the deer to make his appearance. If he wounds the deer, he may stalk it for a distance and then carry it out, and there is solid exercise there. But it is sporadic, occasional, unsystematic, and as far as conditioning is concerned, just about as worthless as a nap on the living-room sofa.

Golf

Probably the third most popular participation exercise is golf. Millions of Americans go to the links on week ends, far more than ever before, and the number increases every year. For the majority, who don't use golf carts, golf has a solid element of exercise. After all, a man who plays eighteen holes will walk approximately four miles, and although the walk is frequently interrupted by addressing a golf ball or lining up a putt or waiting on the tee or green for the foursome ahead to move on, nevertheless there is some element of conditioning in playing eighteen holes of golf, *provided you walk*. But as many eminent heart specialists have observed, eighteen holes of golf is far inferior to four miles of walking, which you can easily do in less than half the time and which gives the clear advantage over golf of *continuous, uninterrupted* exercise that provides real conditioning. Golfing does have more positive than negative aspects, but only a few more.

Another thing to consider is the tension in golf—emotional and sometimes even intellectual tension. The frustration of a bad shot, a shank or a slice or a hook, of losing your ball or topping your ball, or of missing a two-foot putt—all these frustrations and disappointments counteract the relaxing, swinging joy that you get from steady, striding walking.

Of course if you have a relaxed temperament those bad shots and missed putts don't bother you and you can laugh them off. But if frustrations get to you and affect your physical well-being, you should forget golf.

Tennis

The other great sport that is gathering a tremendous head of steam and that appeals to all generations is tennis. Tennis has advantages and disadvantages as compared with golf and many disadvantages as compared to walking or running. Tennis can give you a hard workout in a relatively short period of time. You run in tennis, you swing the racket hard, you move back and forward over the court, you enjoy the challenge of competition. But tennis has the same fatal weakness as far as conditioning is concerned that golf has: you rarely engage in sustained volleying for more than twenty or thirty seconds, and even that is a long series of exchanges. Usually the exchanges cover less than ten seconds even for reasonably good players, and between volleys you stand motionless, idle, with muscles inactive, with no challenge for the circulatory system or the heart.

And tennis too has its frustrations. The double fault. The ball that you're sure you hit in but your opponent is sure you didn't. Or the ball that you're sure your opponent did not hit in but he thinks he did. The direct frustration of competition with somebody who wants to beat you and whom you want to beat.

For many people this is part of the joy of life, the kind of competition they can enjoy as a healthy, even a friendly sort of duel. If you have this kind of temperament, go to it; you'll enjoy tennis and tennis will help you. Though a set of tennis won't help you nearly as much as a two-mile run, it will probably do you more good than harm. But again, if those competitive frustrations get to you, if it's physical condition you're interested in, if you want to avoid difficulties with your heart and circulatory system, then tennis shouldn't be your choice.

Other Rackets

Badminton is very much akin to tennis. Somehow, perhaps because we Americans are not generally that good at badminton, people don't take it seriously. For that reason the do-or-die competition and the resulting frustrations are undoubtedly less. Yet in terms of its activity badminton is close to tennis—swinging the racket, moving back and forth, waiting between shots. It offers about the same advantages and disadvantages, frustrations and rewards that tennis does. If you can take your badminton as an easygoing, pleasant workout, not worrying about whether you win or lose and laughing off the bad shots, then it is probably fine for you—still not as good as a good long walk, but not bad either. But if you are a competitive badminton player, the tension and stress you develop may be too high a price to pay. It may do you more harm than good.

In recent years ping-pong, or table tennis, has caught on. This too provides some exercise—moving around the table, batting the ball back and forth—but it is distinctly inferior to tennis or badminton because you simply don't run as much.

If you're a top-flight player, you can get a good workout playing table tennis. Anybody who watched that marvelous Chinese team must recognize that this can be real physical conditioning. But not one American player in fifty is dedicated enough to get that kind of workout. So unless you're going to really take table tennis seriously and go all out in it, it is unlikely to provide any kind of conditioning. It may be fun, it may be a diversion, it may get your mind off other things, but a conditioner it is not.

Probably the best conditioner of any of the racket games is squash. It's possible for a squash rackets player who is only fair to keep the ball in play for a rather long period, which means that he has to do quite a bit of sustained running and hitting between periods of rest.

As in competitive tennis, in squash the competition can cause frustration and tension. But it can also provide some genuine endurance training.

Even better than squash is handball, a nonracket game which is supposedly related. In handball too it seems that even the beginner quickly acquires an ability to keep the play going for long enough periods so that there can be some sustained benefits.

Once again I doubt very much if these sports can compare in conditioning with an easy two-mile run or even a vigorous four-mile walk. And there are the frustrations of competition that some temperaments can't take without serious tension.

Setting-up Exercises

To stay in the gym for just another minute or two, calisthenics are engaged in by millions of Americans, male and female, of all ages and both sexes. Calisthenics have their purpose, but believe me as an old calisthenics aficionado, conditioning is not one of their purposes. These exercises will tone up your muscles, they will give you the cosmetic appearance of well-defined, sharp muscles in just about any part of the anatomy you choose if you do them enough. But there simply isn't a calisthenic yet devised that will provide real conditioning. Exercises just aren't that sustained.

Since I was fourteen years old I have done calisthenics nearly every morning of my life. I now do two hundred and fifty push-ups every morning, but I space them out—sixty push-ups, then other exercises, then sixty more, then other exercises, then sixty more, then other exercises, then end up with seventy.

There are other exercises that pit one muscle against another, what Charles Atlas used to call dynamic-tension exercises to develop the muscles of the neck, the arms, the shoulders, the chest, legs. I do these too.

They'll make you look much better in a bathing suit, they'll make you stronger, and they'll make you feel better at least psychologically. But they do practically nothing for your heart or circulatory system. Some authorities believe that they may even build up tensions that could be somewhat counterproductive if they're overdone.

Weight Lifting and Boxing

If you are interested primarily in looking good and developing a muscular physique that will be the envy of the block, weight lifting may be your cup of tea.

Weight lifting will build your body, but it will do nothing for the circulatory system or the heart. It is not a conditioner and I don't know of anybody who has ever claimed that it could be. No athlete is more widely respected for power and strength than the world's heavyweight boxing champion, or any boxer for that matter. All through high school and college I boxed almost every day. Instead of the three-minute rounds of the professionals we always boxed two-minute rounds. In those two minutes you could get very tired indeed. Boxing can do good things for your self-confidence, but it is probably the most intense producer of frustration, tension, and fear that mankind has developed. When you're in a boxing ring, you're in there to knock the other man out and he's in there to knock you out. Talk about competition, frustration, tension—boxing is it in spades.

And yet boxers do develop great conditioning. They do it not by boxing, however, but by skipping rope endlessly, which has all the advantages of running if you stay with it the same length of time. And of course the best conditioner of all for boxers is the well-known road work.

George Foreman, Joe Frazier and Muhammed Ali do their five or six miles on the road every day. That is the real conditioner and the reason they're in such superb shape and able to go fifteen three-minute rounds straight.

You can get all the benefits of boxing by running or walking vigorously every day, without paying any of the price in tension, frustration, and fear.

Football

America's two great sports are probably the worst conditioners of all. One outstanding heart specialist contends that in an hour of football a player will consume 2,500 calories. This man is a great heart specialist but he's obviously never played football. If you analyze your activity in football, you find that the actual amount of exercixe is shockingly limited.

In a sixty-minute football game that takes two and a half hours to play, with time outs and the period between halves and so forth, the actual amount of time the ball is in play is only about nine minutes. Considering the fact that these days all the big college and professional teams and many of the high-school teams have separate offensive and defensive platoons, it means that each player plays only four and a half minutes of the two and a half hours the game goes on. When the ball is not in play the men are standing in a huddle or waiting for the ball to be snapped from center—motionless, immobile. The only time the actual play is likely to exceed a few seconds is during a kick-off return; then the entire time will be around fifteen or twenty seconds at most. Obviously under these circumstances there just is not the time to develop any kind of sustained training effect.

There are shocks in football that may be even more vehement than in boxing. When you tackle a man head-on or are tackled by a man head-on, or block or are blocked, you can feel the shock.

At Yale I never missed fall and spring practice, and I played in most of the junior varsity games. This was in the era when we went both ways. If we were put into the game, we weren't allowed to be taken out in the same period unless we stayed out for the rest of that period. My only play with the varsity was very limited indeed. Our captain and tail-back that year was Clint Frank, the best football player in the country, who was recognized as the best when he was awarded the Heisman trophy. On the one play I played for Yale I was put in at right end. Back in the huddle Clint looked at me and my 160 pounds dripping wet and said, "Proxy, you take out Towell." Charlie Towell, the Princeton captain, weighed 260 pounds. He was captain of the wrestling team and he was the biggest man on the field by at least fifty pounds. So when Clint told me I had to block Towell, our other team members almost fell down in the huddle laughing.

Well, when the ball was snapped I did hit Towell, my head

in his midsection. Everything went black and I mean black. Clint gained fifteen or twenty yards on the play and I was immediately taken out. Blackouts, even temporary ones like mine, are rare in football, but that kind of jolting shock is common to almost every play.

Football has the tensions, frustrations, and intense competitiveness of other sports and absolutely none of the conditioning effect. A great sport if you like blocking and tackling —and I loved it—football is anything but a conditioner.

Chances are you don't play football. Fewer and fewer people are doing so and more and more are watching it. But if you're young enough, you may very well be playing touch football for some time. Touch football probably provides far better conditioning than football. Almost every play is a pass play. You run down fifteen or twenty yards for a pass, then have to walk back, and spend very little time in a huddle. There are few if any time outs. But touch football is far, far below distance running or even golf and tennis as a conditioner because there is so much time between actual plays.

Baseball

The sport that provides the poorest conditioning experience of all is probably baseball. The main exercise baseball players get is running from the dugout to their positions, provided they play in the outfield, and then running back in. Baseball has become a very slow game indeed.

Pitchers and catchers get something of a workout, but not the kind of aerobic endurance exercise that running and swimming provide. Throwing a ball hard, as a pitcher does more than a hundred times in a regular nine-inning game, will develop strength in the arms, shoulders, chest, and back but it does nothing in terms of conditioning.

If there's one player on a baseball team who comes close to getting some conditioning, that's a really hustling catcher.

Years ago there was a major-league catcher named Rollie Hemsley who played with a number of different teams. Rollie was Mr. Hustle himself. He was the kind of catcher who, when a batter hit a ball anywhere in the infield, would run down to first base at the same time the batter did, so that if the first baseman missed the ball Rollie could retrieve it and hold the runner on first. In major-league baseball games the first baseman rarely missed a throw, but it did happen occasionally and Hemsley did help hold runners on base. At the same time, in my view, he did more to stay in condition than any other player in the history of the game.

Once in a while an outfielder will make a spectacular catch after a long run of perhaps a hundred feet. Occasionally a batter will hit a triple and have to go all out running the ninety yards from home plate to first, first to second, second to third, and if he's going to make his triple he has to do that in less than nine or ten seconds. But there is no chance to get the kind of aerobic endurance running that requires at least a mile to get even the beginning of a conditioning effect, and even triples are very rare in baseball.

A home run provides no conditioning at all for a player. Once the ball is out of the park, which usually happens by the time the runner is at first base, he simply jogs around the bases. No one can tell me that a hundred-and-twenty-yard jog provides any training effect. On rare occasions there is an inside-the-park home run, which is usually accomplished in less than twelve or thirteen seconds. There is no conditioning effect to that either.

Most of the time the firstbaseman, secondbaseman, shortstop, thirdbaseman, and the outfielders are simply standing still waiting. If they make a play, it will take less than ten seconds, and usually less than five. The conditioning is nil.

All this does not mean baseball and football players cannot be in shape. They may stay in shape by running before or after each game. The actual play of the game provides zero conditioning.

Bicycling

In recent years bicycling long distances has become popular. Many people consider it superlative exercise. Bicycling is excellent recreation. It brings you close to nature, it enables you to cover long distances in short times, and it's a great way to get to work without polluting the atmosphere. But as a conditioner I think it rates far below running or even walking. Theoretically, cycling can be every bit as useful as running or walking. And cycling on a stationary bike in your basement or recreation room or gym, where you pedal continuously for twenty minutes or half an hour, can of course be a superlative conditioner.

But this isn't the way most people cycle. If you watch them you'll see that they sit still, almost motionless, on the down slope of hills, or stop because they have to at stop signs or when the bicycle path is interrupted. They can rarely find a flat, even stretch in which they pedal continuously at a high enough speed to get the kind of exercise that a four-mile-an-hour walk provides.

So bicycle for the fun of it, bicycle for the company of your family or friends, bicycle to get somewhere without polluting the one world we all enjoy. But if aerobic training to help the circulatory system and build the heart is what you're after, forget it.

Skiing and Water Skiing

I remember going skiing when I was twelve years old. In those days we would ski without ski poles and without ski lifts. Skiing consisted of walking herringbone style up a hill and then skiing down. We'd walk up as many hills as we came down. Skiing was a workout then. Today, when people take chair lifts up two or three or four miles and then simply drift down on their skis, they undoubtedly have more fun and more sport, and they need greater technique, skill, coordination, but they don't get aerobic circulatory exercise of any benefit.

A sport that has caught on tremendously in recent years is water skiing—and for good reason. It is exuberant fun to shoot through the water, splashing up the spray behind a speedboat, and the tension on legs and arms undoubtedly requires strength and builds strength. But there's no aerobic training effect whatsoever, no matter how long it's done. Anybody who feels that this is exercise, that it aids the circulatory system, is kidding himself.

Soccer, Basketball, Rowing

Running, walking, and swimming are not the only ways to get aerobic training. I think they're by far the best and the most convenient, but there are other ways, some of which involve vigorous competition but which are predominantly endurance sports. One of these certainly is soccer football. Obviously a goalie and perhaps a back in soccer football get very little exercise, but a forward or a center is running almost all the time. And this is just what the doctor ordered for the heart and circulatory system.

Basketball, provided there aren't too many substitutions, is another sport that gives some excellent aerobic training, if played on a sustained basis with few time outs and for periods of fifteen or twenty minutes at a time.

One of the most remarkably disciplined challenges for the human body, involving terrific aerobic training, is crew. Over the right distance a crew race can take twenty minutes and twenty minutes of hard, exhausting, continuous endurance exercise. Maybe this is one of the reasons why a recent study of Harvard and Yale crews over a period of years showed that they lived an average of more than six years longer than their classmates. I suspect that their longevity may have been more related to the fact that they took some pride in the condition they developed and that they continued their sports activity. They may have done single scull rowing or switched to more popular sports like walking, hiking, and possibly some running in their later years.

The study was conducted by Dr. Curtis Prout, who practices internal medicine at the Harvard University Health Center. Prout did the study partly because school folklore had led to an impression that oarsmen die younger than other students because of the rigorous training, sustained exertion, and precise timing that crew requires. Also, the *Journal of the American Medical Association* had published (in 1968) a letter stating that "the members of the Harvard Crew of 1948 have all since died of various cardiac diseases."

Dr. Prout says, "That statement was hotly denied by every one of them."

The Prout Study included 172 oarsmen at Harvard and Yale, each of whom rowed at least once in the four-mile varsity race between the two colleges, and an equal number of classmates for purposes of comparison.

"At both Yale and Harvard the average life-span for the crew was higher than for controls," Dr. Prout reported.

The Yale crew members lived 6.35 years longer than their New Haven classmates, and the Harvard crew members survived 6.24 years longer than their Cambridge classmates.

The studies were made of men who graduated from Yale and Harvard in the 1870's and 1880's. It was made of athletes that long ago because it was necessary that all had deceased to make the study comprehensive and complete.

Hockey is another sport that can provide solid endurance training. This is probably much less true of professional hockey or even first-class college hockey, because the substitutions are so frequent that the forwards, who get the most exercise, are taken out after two or three minutes of hard play. Hockey for conditioning is usually the kind of hockey that one plays in pickup games or in the ice hockey we used to like at the Winter Club in Lake Forest, Illinois, when I was a child. We'd play for hours at a time.

This certainly provides an opportunity for aerobic training because you're constantly moving on your skates. Exertion is steady and the crisp, cool air of winter enables you to keep at it far longer than most summer sports.

Cross-Country Skiing

Apparently the best conditioner of all, according to aficionados of endurance, is cross-country skiing. Unfortunately this is a rare sport. Very few people engage in it in this country, although a few more are getting into it every year. The country where it is most popular is Norway. In a recent Olympics the first six finishers in the cross-country ski race were Norwegians.

Perhaps this is the reason Norway is the only country in the world in which the men outlive the women. It's one of the few countries in which you really have a massive, population-wide sport participation, and the endurance sport of cross-country skiing is high on the Norwegians' list of favorites.

To sum up, *enjoy* whatever sport turns you on. Whatever makes you happy and relaxed. Whatever skill you have developed and gives you satisfaction. There are other values in life besides longevity, good circulation, and a strong heart. But if it's good solid internal health you're interested in, running, walking, or swimming should probably be your choice.

VI· DIET

125

16 · The Joy of Eating

DOCTORS, NUTRITIONISTS, and food experts warn us continually about foods that may be harmful to our health. In fact the warnings about what we shouldn't eat sometimes seem so widespread that we begin to feel that "everything we enjoy is either illegal, immoral, or fattening."

Fortunately, this is not really true. There are a great many delicious foods that are low in calories. Also, I think you can allow yourself an occasional high-calorie treat. I believe it is absolutely essential that you enjoy what you eat, that you satisfy your taste buds and that you look forward to eating. Eating is a pleasure that you can savor in anticipation, enjoy while you are indulging it, and relish later in your memory. And we can enjoy it from the time we are small children until we are very old indeed. It is truly one of the great pleasures of life.

It is perfectly consistent to place a high value on the enjoyment of food and still manage to be lean and healthy. One way to achieve this is to adopt a program of vigorous exercise. I suppose I don't have to say that I recommend this highly because of all the other benefits exercise gives. But it's perfectly possible to enjoy eating, remain lean, and not exercise very much. I don't advise it because I feel that exercise can be such a useful, happy part of the healthy life. But ultimately the choice is yours.

Eat for Pleasure and Health

We like so many foods that are good for us that they should be the starting place of any diet plan we adopt. Almost all of us enjoy fresh, juicy oranges, apples, melons, and other fresh fruits. It's no accident that the Garden of Eden and the legendary dwelling places of the gods were laden with tasty fruit. I can't think of any fruit that doesn't offer nutritional benefit as well as solid enjoyment. Eating fruit is a good way to get the unrefined sugar and some of the vitamins and minerals our bodies need. Fruit juices too are tasty and beneficial.

Lean meats, especially chicken, fish and veal, are high in protein and low in calories. What's more, they can be prepared in many delicious low-calorie ways.

Most Americans are not vegetable eaters, but I feel sure that when you experiment with the wide variety of fresh and frozen vegetables you'll find quite a few that you really enjoy. As the Senator from Wisconsin, I feel it only just to point out that there are two dairy foods all nutritionists recommend, cottage cheese and skim milk.

Most of the bread baked by commercial bakers is a nutritional disaster, but there are several new kinds that are delicious and loaded with food value. My special favorite is sprouted-wheat bread.

I can honestly say that I enjoy food more now than ever. I am more aware of tastes and textures and I savor things more.

Moderation Increases Enjoyment

One of the best motivations for a moderate approach to eating—thus getting your weight down and keeping it down—seems the most contradictory at first. That is that it increases the pleasure of eating. You may say, Senator Proxmire, what are you talking about? Are you out of your head? That is exactly what I'm trying to escape.

But that isn't true.

Just think about it. It is virtually impossible to really enjoy food unless you're hungry. And the hungrier you are the better food tastes. I have found that the simplest, plainest food can be really delicious, and I mean satisfying in every respect, if I am hungry. A simple plate of sliced tomatoes with nothing but a little salt and pepper can be a wonderful taste treat.

Everyone has had the experience of eating when he wasn't hungry and not noticing what he was eating. Sometimes we eat a whole meal almost without realizing it. But when you're hungry, a simple hamburger, a dish of green beans, or a glass of grapefruit juice will hit the spot. It will taste so good you'll be surprised.

If you follow the hold-your-weight-down prescription, food will almost always taste good, because you are hungry when you eat and you stop when you're not. You will notice this change immediately. You simply get more sheer enjoyable satisfaction in your taste buds. The way to do this is to stop eating as soon as your hunger is satisfied, or maybe even a little before it's fully satisfied.

My father, who was a doctor—a general practitioner—used to suggest that everyone should walk away from the table at least a little hungry. And he knew what he was talking about, because at the age of forty-five, when he weighed two hundred pounds, he decided he had to do something about it. He was six feet tall, but he decided that he was fat and soft and in the next year he lost thirty pounds. He stayed at that weight for the rest of his life, which was a long, long time. He knew what obesity, even mild obesity, could do, not only to shorten life but to make the older years a time of senility and dependence. My father was a happy, healthy, vigorous man who carried on a busy medical practice twelve hours a day, seven days a week, fifty-two weeks a year, until he died at the age of seventy-eight. He was independent and he enjoyed life.

The final happy answer to all this is that holding your weight down and watching your diet, making it a daily habit, is going to give you far more enjoyment of food than if you don't. It's a well-known fact that too much of anything decreases our pleasure in it. The joy of eating will be yours again when you eat moderately.

When you recognize that, understand it, and believe it, you can't miss.

17 · The American Diet: What's Wrong with It

ENJOYING FOOD is important, but most of us will have to retrain our appetites if we are going to eat the healthy diet our bodies require. Americans have developed a number of very bad eating habits over the past few decades. Nutritionists and diet specialists agree on this, and they also agree that the most serious and dangerous faults in American eating habits are that we eat too much refined sugar products, with very little food value, and too much fat.

Most people today get all the sugar they need by eating fruits and vegetables, which contain sugar and starches combined with vitamins and minerals. Refined sugar, the sugar we add to foods, consists of empty calories. It provides the body with energy but it offers no other nutrients. And we eat much too much of it in candies, soft drinks, cookies, cakes and pies. Our bodies cannot handle the amounts of sugar we eat and we eventually cause serious damage if we continue to eat it.

The case against refined sugar has made a strong impression on me and I have cut way down on my intake, although I have a very sweet tooth. I must admit that I like few things better than ice cream, and I could eat a quart at a time. Cookies and candies are something I find hard to resist, and cherry pie—wow! Nevertheless, I've forsworn all these things—except for an occasional indulgence—because the experts have convinced me I will pay too high a price in the long run for the temporary pleasure they give me.

I don't think foods made with refined sugar should be avoided at all times. An occasional piece of candy, an ice-cream sundae once a month, even a soft drink once in a great while won't kill you. But eating these things should not be a habit. Try to eat them as infrequently as possible.

The Staff of Life?

In spite of all the silly television commercials about what bread will do for you, every scrap of scientific information I've seen indicates that with very few exceptions American commercial bread offers almost nothing in the way of nutrients. The rise of interest in health foods has caused several companies to bring out healthful breads—I've already mentioned sprouted-wheat bread—but these are rare exceptions. Since most commercial bread offers so little food value, I would suggest eliminating it from your diet.

Breakfast—Cholesterol Unlimited

If ever there was a meal designed to foster and encourage heart attacks, it is the typical American breakfast. Almost everything in it is wrong as far as holding down cholesterol and being good to your heart is concerned. The lone innocent that stands out from a sea of cholesterol-producing products is fruit juice. If you have orange juice, grapefruit juice, or some other juice that's great. After that it's usually downhill all the way. Hot or cold cereal served with cream is bad considering the cholesterol-producing elements in cream. Bacon and eggs are both foods that should be eaten sparingly by anyone watching his or her cholesterol level. Commercial bread and butter is another no-no. (In Chapters 19 and 20, those on my own diet and on the food experts, we'll discuss breakfasts that are good for you.)

What About Cold Cereals?

We have been brainwashed so much on television about the virtues of breakfast cereals that many of us think they really must be healthful.

The answer to that one was brilliantly supplied to a United States Senate committee when Dr. Robert Choate, chairman of the Council on Children, Media and Merchandising, appeared before the Senate Commerce Committee. Here is a portion of Dr. Choate's testimony on an experiment by Dr. William Caster, professor of nutrition at the University of Georgia, who carried on experiments involving popular cereals and their ability to support life in rats.

Said Choate, "He recognized the milk-must-be-added arguments of the cereal company nutritionists who appeared here in August of 1970 and he asked students to grind up the cardboard front of some of the cereal boxes and to add sugar, milk and raisins and feed the mixture to a group of rats."

It was found that the cardboard box with milk and raisins and sugar would allow some growth, and was definitely superior to some popular breakfast cereals. Dr. Choate ended his comments with this statement: "When cardboard, which is normally thrown away, provides more nourishment than processed grains at sixty or eighty cents a pound, I think it is time to take a second look at who shapes the nation's nutrition."

So much for the food value of many of the cereals you and I see advertised as just what we and our children need for glowing good health.

Coffee Breaks

Another nutritional disaster on the American scene is the coffee break in homes, offices and factories, in which people drink coffee liberally sweetened with sugar and eat a sweet roll, a Danish, or a piece of coffee cake. If you add cream to your coffee, it makes it that much worse. A meal or snack of coffee and a sweet roll has almost no food value, yet such snacks are consumed by literally tens of millions of Americans every day and often more than once a day. Almost all the calories in these foods are empty calories. They make you fat but they provide virtually no useful nutrients or vitamins. Such eating habits constitute a road to weakness, disability, and obesity.

Once-in-a-Whiles

There are some foods that are good for us if we eat them once in a while. Most of these are reasonably high in fat and cholesterol, but they are rich in food value. Try to make them regular if infrequent—once a week is a pretty good habit. Liver is probably the most important of these. It contains just about everything you need for a rich blood supply and for a whole series of vitamins and minerals. Eggs are an excellent protein source, but they have such a high cholesterol content that once a week is probably often enough for a couple of eggs. A lean steak is fine too, provided it's a once-a-week treat. Nuts and peanut butter are delicious—great favorites of mine—but they are both caloric bombs. I try to avoid them except very occasionally.

Snacks?

How about snacks? One expert on heart disease has concluded from a study that there is an inverse relationship between the number of times one eats and the likelihood of heart attack. He found by far the highest heart attack rate among those who have one meal a day, somewhat less among those who have two, less among those who have three, and substantially less among those who have four. People who eat as many as six meals a day have the least.

Naturally, this was on the basis of equalizing the number of calories. A person who has six light, small meals a day consumes very little each time, and is less likely to have heart trouble than one who has one very large meal. This makes sense because of the burden that digestion can put on the heart and also because of the lack of balance that one heavy meal is likely to have. There are several things to consider about snacks.

The big problem, of course, is how to avoid excessive caloric consumption by giving in to the "eat often" scenario.

This way you eat often and you eat the food that is good for you and that you enjoy. It keeps you filled and happy, and by carefully following your scale and your calorie counter you keep the whole thing under control.

It's especially important to avoid the most common "snack." Millions of Americans go after work to the local tavern for beers, or go home to have cocktails with their spouses. There is no question that this is a pleasant interlude; for some it is the high point in the day. Maybe you just won't give it up for anything. But consider the possibility of giving up that cocktail or two or three. The calories you consume are dead, strictly negative.

In my view this cocktail hour is the single most destructive habit in the civilized world, destructive of health for millions of people because it becomes compulsive. It can also destroy jobs and families, and it leads to tens of thousands of deaths on the highways. Of the 50,000 people killed on the roads every year, it is said that some 35,000 are killed because the driver causing the accident is under the influence of alcohol.

Substitute Exercise for Cocktails

What a great improvement in the health, wellbeing, and I think overall happiness of our country if the cocktail hour became an exercise hour! We would have not only a stronger, leaner country but a far happier one. I'm convinced that the best prescription for a better country would be individual determination to end that cocktail hour.

We tried Prohibition and it failed dismally. I'm convinced that this is something we should not try to do by law, but something we can do by example. Believe me, life can be fuller, happier, even during the hour itself, if we exercise, swim, walk, run, than if we wrap ourselves around beers or martinis.

TV Plus Snacks Equals Fat

A second, far less serious weakness, certainly less serious in terms of violent accidents than mixing alcohol and gasoline, is mixing TV with snacks. It is said that the typical American spends more time watching TV than anything else except possibly working and sleeping. And for many Americans more time is spent watching TV than either working or sleeping.

Television has become a part of life and it's going to remain so in America for many decades to come. There is no reason why it can't be an entertaining, edifying, educational experience. It usually isn't. But it can be in the future, especially if you select programs carefully and don't become a TV addict.

What concerns me in this book, however, is that TV mixed with a snack can be a killer. A friend of mine who is an important Washington personality, and also one of the biggest, fattest men I've ever known, literally destroyed his health, not by eating too much at meals, but by turning on the TV every night at 9:00 P.M. and for four hours sitting and watching it with a huge bowl constantly kept full of popcorn and quarts of melted butter.

For some it's cheese crackers, potato chips, candy, cookies, soft drinks, and all kinds of dead, nothing foods.

What makes this such a deadly habit is the regularity of

it, the fact that so many will spend literally every evening this way. Once in a while, maybe once a week or once a month, an evening of TV and a few snacks will do no harm. But there are probably as many untimely deaths caused by overeating before TV as are caused by mixing booze and high-speed driving.

18 · Keep Your Weight Down

YOU MAY VERY WELL be digging your grave with your teeth. Doctors and nutritionists are finding that Americans—even middle-class Americans—suffer from poor nutrition and just plain malnutrition. Although the science of nutrition is not as fully developed as it might be, there doesn't seem to be any doubt about certain facts. The data indicating that obesity is a major culprit in causing disease is now overwhelming.

But that's not all. If you're going to be healthy, you must eat a *balanced* diet. You will have to consume regularly some clearly required nutrients, vitamins, and minerals.

Balance Essential

We do know what a balanced diet is. You need one or more servings a day from the four basic food groups: milk, meat, vegetable-fruit, and bread-cereal. If you keep to that balance and hold down your calories you have it made. And yet for most of us the contradictory arguments on dieting are confusing.

There are sharp differences between the nutritionists who emphasize eating a balanced diet, eating the right kinds of foods, getting sufficient vitamins, minerals, and so forth, and the dieters who contend that the important thing is to hold down your caloric intake.

Now of course the right answer is to accept the advice of

both, to eat a limited diet but a balanced and nutritious diet with all the necessary vitamins and minerals, and there's no conflict between them.

But let's face it, we are human. There's a tendency for us to eat too much of even the foods that are good for us. One of the rationalizations I find hard to resist when I confront a tempting fruit salad or veal, chicken, skimmed milk, fish, or any number of other things which are sound and good nutritionally, is that certainly this is the kind of food my system needs to make me strong and healthy. Therefore why not go ahead and indulge my appetite to the fullest? The answer is that the time comes rather quickly when eating even the best and most nutritious food is really counterproductive; you are far, far healthier if you limit the amount ruthlessly and stay there.

You might remind yourself to underline your resolve to say NO. Obesity, debility, and death can result from a perfectly balanced diet containing none of the dead foods, if we overeat.

The Long, Long Pull

The big point in weight control is exactly that—controlling your weight, keeping your weight down. One of the easiest actions in the world is to go on a diet for a short time, a day or two or three or four. It's something else to stay on that diet for weeks and even months. And it's something else too to adopt weight control as a way of life for the rest of your life. But this is exactly what you should do. And this is by far the hardest kind of diet action to take. It's one for which all the suggestions in this chapter on no-nos should provide reinforcement.

Once again the big point is not taking weight off; the big point is keeping weight off, holding it off, staying with your balanced diet every day, at every meal, from now on.

The rewards in better health, in vitality, in preventing

heart disease and stroke, and in promoting the general day-to-day good, happy feeling of health makes exerting control well worth it.

Adlai Stevenson used to say that patriotism should not be confused with the emotional ecstasy of the moment when our hearts swell with pride as we see the flag or hear "The Star-Spangled Banner" or watch a parade. Patriotism is not a matter of a momentary paroxysm of pride and joy in our great country. Patriotism is a matter of the long, quiet dedication of a lifetime, the constant furthering of the best interests of our country in every way we can find to do it.

Similarly, winning the battle of weight control is not a matter of the paroxysm of a fast. It's one thing to give up a single meal or even a whole day of meals. This can be a very valuable adjunct to dieting and a perfectly proper recourse when done thoughtfully and under the guidance of a physician (see Chapter 24, on fasting), but this kind of quick weight loss is not to be confused with the far more important adaptation of moderate, limited eating for a better life.

How Much Should You Weigh?

One doctor who has studied weight for many years argues that it's not satisfactory to be the same weight when you're forty-five or fifty or sixty that you were when you were twenty-five. This disagrees with a widely held theory that your weight at twenty-five is your ideal weight. How many times have you heard the boast, "I don't weigh an ounce more than I weighed when I was twenty-five?"

Because most people lead sedentary lives and their muscle mass diminishes, this weight expert argues that you should *lose* every year after you're thirty. He argues that when you're forty years old you should weigh 5 percent less than when you are twenty-five, provided you were not obese and were healthy and reasonably lean at that age.

Now prepare for another shock. At fifty you should lose another 5 percent, and at sixty another 5 percent!

I've tried to follow this prescription and I've come pretty close to it. When I went into the army in World War II, at the age of twenty-five, I was six feet tall and weighed 163 pounds. When I got out at the age of thirty I weighed the same. Because I had continued to exercise after college, I was in reasonably good shape while I was in the service. I could be classified as lean.

Until I was well into my fifties I was five pounds below that so-called ideal weight; that is, I weighed about 158 pounds. Then I decided to comply with the formula of losing 5 percent of what my weight was at twenty-five. I calculated that ideally I should weigh 155 at the age of forty, 147 at the age of fifty, and about 140 at the age of sixty. Shortly after my fifty-sixth birthday I began to lose, and I went down to 143. So I'm right on schedule to reach 140 at the age of sixty. I'm lean and light, and I never felt better in my life. In fact, if I felt any better I'd be dangerous.

Any mechanical formula of this kind can be wrong, and it might be very wrong indeed, depending on what you weighed when you were twenty-five or thirty. The loss of 5 percent of your weight a decade after you're thirty would probably make a lot less sense for women than it would for men. But it has worked out very well for me and it might for you. Talk it over with your doctor, of course, before you adopt this ambitious goal. Furthermore, unless you know a lot about your self-control, and unless you have found that you can stick with a diet and a long exercise program, such a goal may be too much for you even if the weight would be ideal for your heart and circulatory system.

19 · My Own Diet

MY OWN DIET may seem absolutely impossible for you, or maybe it will intrigue and attract you. I find it delicious and satisfying as well as nutritionally sound.

For breakfast I have a ten-ounce glass of freshly squeezed orange juice, a three-ounce serving of a protein dish—tuna fish or herring or beef or chicken breasts—and two slices of lightly buttered sprouted-wheat bread toast. In addition I have eight ounces of skim milk mixed with an ounce of wheat germ. That's enough to make any nutritionist jump with unrestricted joy. This breakfast gives me staying power. I find that I no longer get that empty feeling at midmorning.

I usually have lunch in the Senate dining room. Usually I have a fruit plate, and it's a delicious treat. It consists of sections of grapefruit and orange (an entire orange and at least half a large grapefruit) on a bed of lettuce with two or three prunes, sections of apple, ten or fifteen strawberries or some slices of cantaloupe or honeydew, and four ounces of cottage cheese. Believe me, this is a mouth-watering combination. It's also very filling. On days when my scale says yes, I also have a large bowl of whatever soup is available. Soup is a great favorite of mine.

That's my lunch—filling, delicious, jam-packed with almost every kind of vitamin. It may be that this is a cultivated taste—I don't think I always liked cottage cheese. But when you wrap that cottage cheese around a strawberry or orange section there are few thing that taste better. And cottage cheese and melon—ah! nectar of the gods.

Although that fruit salad is my stand-by, occasionally, maybe once a week, I have filet of sole or broiled trout or liver. Another lunch variation is what the Senate dining room calls Banana Tropicale, which is a banana split down the middle, filled with peanut butter, surrounded with prunes stuffed with cottage cheese, and served on lettuce. It's very tasty indeed.

In the middle of the afternoon, about 3:30, I have an apple as a snack, a hard Western Delicious. And it hits the spot.

For dinner I have a variety of delicious fish. I can feast on sole, cod, haddock, trout, or fish sticks. Sometimes I have veal, sometimes chicken breasts, occasionally liver, and once in a while a filet mignon or butt steak.

In each case I carefully consult the calorie counter and keep the amount of meat consumption between 250 and 450 calories.

I find the calorie counter absolutely essential. It is no trick for me to eat 1,500 calories of steak at one sitting without feeling full. But since I cut it down to 400 or 450 calories I've found that I get almost the same enjoyment by simply taking a little longer to eat, and that it's possible to hold down the caloric intake while getting a far better balance in dinner.

In recent years the food industry has done a marvelous job of packaging frozen vegetables. They come on strong with new Japanese, Chinese, and Italian frozen vegetables, frozen peas, string beans, carrots, succotash—whatever suits your palate. But if your food budget is important, canned vegetables are just about as healthy, if a little less colorful and tasty. They are cheap and nutritious.

The portions can be generous without contributing many calories, and such vegetables provide a balance and a bulk that your system needs regularly for vitality and health.

Potatoes are something I do without, although I know the overwhelming majority of my fellow Americans rarely eat lunch or dinner without them. I have nothing against potatoes and the jackets are very nourishing indeed. They are cheap and nutritious. It's just that I always want to add butter or sour cream, which greatly increases the calories in the serving and adds to the fat and cholesterol content.

My favorite dinner beverage is V-8 juice. Sometimes if my weight is up a little I simply drink water. Once in a while I drink skim milk or some tasty fruit juice.

I try hard to avoid dessert, although I don't always succeed.

I Love It

Frankly, I've never enjoyed food more than I do now. It has never tasted better. I find genuine, epicurean, physical joy in eating. And I have been able to do this while holding my weight down, not only by exercising but also by watching the calorie counter and the scale carefully and regularly, and by concentrating on those foods that taste good but aren't fattening.

The pleasure of eating has been greatly enhanced by the generous use of lemon juice on fish, on vegetables, and in V-8 juice, by occasional lapses into tartar sauce to make the fish taste better, and by a tasty, very low-calorie treat I have found, which is both filling and wholesome—celery stalks and carrot sticks with a dip of ketchup and lemon juice occasionally dolled up with a dash of horseradish. This is a diet I'm able to stick to four to seven days a week as a regular staple diet.

As a senator I'm often on the road traveling. When I am I have to eat restaurant meals, and this can be a real problem. Sometimes the answer is to take cans of sardines and tuna with me and eat them in my hotel room along with sunflower seeds and fruit bought at a local grocery store.

Banquet Eating

It's not difficult at all for a senator who is invited to a banquet to eat nothing. No one is offended; almost everyone has the good sense to realize that you probably had to attend another banquet or eat elsewhere. Once in a while I go to a good restaurant and eat the usual—steak, potatoes, salad. It would be murder if I ate such meals regularly, but it's infrequent enough so that it affects neither my scale nor the balance of my dietary consumption.

Find the Right Diet for You

I certainly don't offer my diet as one that everybody in the country should follow. It is strictly a suggestion. It may be that you could not possibly follow the same diet without feeling sentenced to a life totally minus the joy of indulging your taste buds. Some of the foods I eat may turn you off so completely that you feel you'd rather be a fat, tired, irritable, short-lived wreck than eat like that.

I have two answers to this. In the first place, you may find that if you follow this kind of diet you'll cultivate a taste for it very quickly. In the second place, it's easy to develop a similar healthy diet that will offer equal nutritive value and balance, and will fill you up without putting on weight. It can be done with a little ingenuity, and maybe the diet I've suggested can serve as the framework.

I Ate the Whole Thing

Sometimes it is good to relax your restrictions and eat what you want.

One day last June the Senate had an all-day harangue. I was involved in a fight with the budget director in the subcommittee I chair on foreign aid. I had a bitter exchange with colleagues on the Senate floor, in which I charged that the Defense Department had deliberately insulted the Appropriations Committee by refusing to send a witness. All this had delayed me from leaving the Senate until 8:00 P.M.

When I left I had less than an hour to get to the grocery store, almost five miles from the Capitol and a short distance from my house. On the way home I thought, Why not just relax and let the diet go?

I did. I bought eight ounces of filet mignon, about four ounces more than I usually eat at any one time, and listen to this—some pecan-crunch ice milk. Now if there is anything that should be avoided on almost any kind of diet, it seems to me that it's a combination of commercial sugar and fat. Ice milk has both, but I was in the mood to let go.

Home I went, and after eight ounces of that delicious filet mignon and a solid pint of pecan-crunch, topped off with six or eight Ritz crackers smothered in peanut butter, a pint of V-8 juice, a large banana, two graham crackers, and two huge, juicy plums, I felt I'd been as wicked as most guys must feel after a night at Hugh Hefner's Playboy Club, complete with bunnies and booze.

I figured the total calories of that repast at about 1,700, at least twice as much as makes sense in any one meal. Furthermore, the composition was, if not all bad, not good for teeth or heart or much of anything else.

Obviously it was a kind of night on the town, to add all kinds of flab, cholesterol, and misery if repeated more often than once in a rare while. But I must confess, I did it!

20 · Bringing the Experts Together

TWO OF THE OUTSTANDING EXPERTS in the country on what to eat to stay healthy are Adelle Davis, perhaps the most widely recognized and read nutritionist, and Dr. Lawrence Lamb, a syndicated columnist and a brilliant specialist on the relationship between diet and heart disease.

After reading Davis and Lamb you'll see why it's so puzzling and difficult for people like you and me, who are neither doctors nor nutritionists, to determine just exactly what the right kind of diet is.

One of the reasons I have the effrontery to write this book although I am neither a nutritionist nor a doctor is that I think it is useful to apply common sense and the observations of a lifetime to the varying and sometimes conflicting prescriptions of the experts.

Fortunately, a common theme runs through the advice of most nutritionists and doctors. Even experts as diverse as Davis and Lamb agree on the importance of moderation in eating and on the desirability of a balanced diet—balanced in choices from the four essential food groups of dairy products, meat, vegetables-fruit, and bread-cereals. Indeed, I think almost everyone who has studied the effect of food on health would agree that a moderate balanced diet is the right diet for most people, unless they have some unusual illness or deficiency.

Unfortunately, those who have a balanced diet are in a minority. What a human tragedy it is that in this affluent country of ours, so amply endowed with food, so many millions eat so unhealthily! A very large proportion of our people in all income categories are careless, short-sighted, or just plain ignorant about their food habits, and as a result they're in serious nutritional trouble.

One of the reasons I've written this book is to try to persuade more Americans to adopt good food habits for themselves and to try to serve as an example to their children, their relatives, their friends, and their associates of what a healthy, balanced, limited diet can do for you.

Carbohydrates vs. Protein

If you read both Adelle Davis and Lawrence Lamb you may be puzzled and troubled at the differences between them.

Let's look at them. Adelle Davis has a very wide following and properly so. Her books are real eye-openers for anyone interested in nutrition. They are filled with careful analysis and study of the effects of foods and other nutrients on the body.

The fundamental difference in the diets recommended by Adelle Davis and Lawrence Lamb is that Adelle Davis stresses high-protein foods while Lawrence Lamb is a carbohydrate man. He argues that a study of societies with a low incidence of heart attack and other diseases that plague our country have diets largely if not exclusively carbohydrates. He emphasizes fruits and vegetables, and comes down very hard against cholesterol foods and fats.

Lamb feels that the "protein kick" can be and probably is overdone. He favors a significant consumption of protein on a daily basis, but his principal emphasis is on avoiding cholesterol and fat and limiting caloric intake. As far as Lamb is concerned, the leaner you are, the better.

Adelle Davis, on the other hand, emphasizes protein emphatically. In one of the most impressive sections of her book *Let's Eat Right to Keep Fit* she describes seven or eight alternative breakfasts. The first three or four of these breakfasts, based on what most Americans eat, are high in carbohydrates. It is only the last three breakfasts, which are high in protein, that Adelle Davis considers adequate. She cites studies showing that the typical American breakfast is so lacking in protein that the blood-sugar level rises, then falls shortly afterward, and remains low most of the working hours for tens of millions of Americans.

She points out that a simple, inexpensive breakfast can provide the kind of concentrated protein abundance that will carry you through the morning with plenty of vim, vigor, and vitality.

She has an excellent little guide for eating: Breakfast like a king, lunch like a prince, and dine like a pauper.

I think Adelle Davis has an excellent point on the importance of protein for breakfast because protein raises and keeps raised the blood-sugar level so necessary for well-being. I am sure it doesn't contradict the Lamb position, because the protein you need can be ample but limited in terms of caloric content.

At the same time, it's perfectly possible to follow the Lamb prescription of emphasizing carbohydrates for the rest of the day, with fruit salad for lunch, fruit snacks, small protein portions for dinner with ample vegetable portions and a fruit dessert.

One could say that Adelle Davis is likely to keep you energetic and well. Lawrence Lamb is likely to keep you free of the number-one killer, heart attack. Together they make a very happy combination.

21 · The Decline and Fall of American Restaurants

THE LATEST FIGURES show that in America one meal in three is eaten in a restaurant of some kind. This fact is probably the toughest single obstacle to a better diet for the American people.

It's one thing for the housewife to prepare nutritious balanced meals from fruits, fresh vegetables, meat, milk, and other foods. It is something else for most of us to eat that balanced diet in a restaurant.

It is very difficult nowadays to find any restaurant which will serve you healthy food. Thanks to local ordinances, most restaurants won't immediately poison you, but if you were to live on restaurant food long enough, your energy would be sapped and the prospects of illness would be substantially increased. Even if you eat only a certain percentage of your meals in restaurants, you are less healthy and probably much less healthy than you should be.

For instance, it's hard to find a restaurant that will serve any fresh fruit.

Recently I went into a restaurant in Milwaukee that I especially liked because it served a delicious fruit plate. I thought so much of that fruit plate that I used to go out to the kitchen to shake hands with the chef and thank her for doing a masterful, imaginative, and healthy job. Now I discovered that they had discontinued the fruit plate. Why?

Well, the waiter said that not enough people ordered it, and that fruits were too hard to keep without rotting and wasting.

Now you and I know why not enough people ordered that fruit plate. Most Americans in a restaurant think in terms of steak, French fries, and pie.

Has Anybody Seen a Vegetable Lately?

Recently a letter to the *New York Times* complained that it's hard to find a restaurant that serves vegetables. And it is. There is probably no better indication of a good cook than well-prepared vegetables. Vegetables cooked with care and imagination can outshine even the main course.

The trouble is that in most restaurants the vegetables are just thrown in as side dishes, and anyone who runs a restaurant in this computer age knows that he has to economize and what he can economize on.

Most people won't complain if their share of carrots, peas, broccoli, or Brussels sprouts is very small, so small it's not enough to do anybody any good. You might complain about a small serving of steak or lobster or hamburger, but most people have come to feel that the vegetable is there just to provide a different color or aroma. What a shame, when vegetables can be so tasty, so delicious, so healthy.

Many a restaurant serves nothing but steak, baked potato, booze, and pastry. This formula for a living death is the backbone of the restaurant industry. You may be able to order other dishes, but this is what they push and feature on the menu and what you're expected to get. It undoubtedly shortens the life of Americans by years, by millions of man years, and increases the medical bill by billions of dollars.

Some health restaurants are beginning to develop, but in my opinion it will be a long time before they flourish.

Bring Your Lunch to Work

Meanwhile, what do you do if you work from 9:00 A.M. until 5:00 or 6:00 P.M. in an office or from 7:00 A.M. until 3:30 P.M. in a factory? Go without lunch?

You can try to work out an arrangement for nutritious meals with the place where you regularly eat, whether it's the company cafeteria or a restaurant in which you can get on good terms with the proprietor. However, it's probably easier and wiser to join the legion of people who bring their own lunch to work in a paper bag or briefcase. I think you'll find that you can save hundreds of dollars a year this way and have a much healthier life. You can bring fruit, cottage cheese, and even some of the sunflower seeds Adelle Davis recommends so highly.

And in a Thermos you can bring V-8 juice, skim milk, orange juice, apple juice. Bring your own sandwiches made with sprouted-wheat or one of the other good health breads. If you want to refrigerate part of your food you can usually work out some kind of arrangement at the office. A surprising number of offices have refrigerators. If not, perhaps the company cafeteria staff will put your lunch in their refrigerator, or even a nearby friendly restaurant may cooperate if you buy milk and soup there.

22 · How to Say *No*

DAVID FROST, the delightful TV host, recently invited a group of "beautiful people" to accompany him on a flight from New York to Bermuda. He had some of the leading movers and shakers in this country, outstanding economists, businessmen, senators, governors, movie actors and actresses. When Frost and his group arrived in Bermuda, they went to one of those lovely Bermuda pools and changed into their swimming suits to enjoy the warm sun of that idyllic island.

After observing the men in their swimming trunks a forthright guest said, "Why is it that almost all the men these days look as if they were pregnant?" The answer is that they don't know how to say NO to all the tasty food thrust before them.

For some strange reason, almost nobody who writes on taking off weight tells you really effective ways to say NO.

For years I've read every article in newspapers and magazines, and every book I could get my hands on, about dieting. We've been swamped by diets of all kinds, advice from doctors and nutritionists, and exercises by the score. I cannot remember running across much straightforward advice on exactly how to say NO and keep saying NO to tempting food when you're hungry, and NO to eating more than you should day after day. In this chapter and the next I will do just that.

It's one thing to take off weight. Almost everybody has

done that, and can do it without a great deal of difficulty. I must say again that the problem is not how to take off weight but how to keep it off year after year. And this is *much* more difficult than most diet prescribers admit. It's one of the hardest things I can think of. It's far tougher for a normal, healthy adult to keep his weight down than it is to cut out smoking and drinking, even if these are ingrained habits.

Toughest Test of Will

Dieting may easily be the toughest test of our will that we encounter in this day and age. Almost all of us have more food available than is good for us.

In this chapter I want to give you the best advice I can on how to achieve the ability to say no and how to continue to say no as long as you live. I want to give you this advice because I couldn't find it anywhere, so I had to develop my own techniques. As a healthy, hungry adult who loves to eat, I found saying no tough at first, and now that I've learned some helpful facts I want to share them.

And how we need such knowledge! Far too many people go back and forth between weight loss and weight gain. They go down for a month or two months but they come back up after a month or two months. How often have you or any of your friends who have tried to lose weight been successful in keeping that weight off year after year?

Age Is No Excuse

Obesity—especially after the age of thirty—is so common in this country that the nonobese person is considered strange.

I once talked to a tailor in Sun Prairie, Wisconsin, who had a theory that all men above the age of forty had to endure an expanded waistline because there was something about their tissues that naturally bloated. If this didn't happen there was something unnatural and wrong. But I've been able to get back to that stage of the whipcord stomach at the age of fifty-seven, and there's no medical reason why others who want to do the same thing cannot do so. It isn't easy, but believe me, it's possible.

Think how appalling it is that almost all Americans over twenty or twenty-five years of age are already too fat. Recent research has found that there is nothing, and I mean nothing on earth, that is more certainly and universally destructive of health than obesity.

We are a fat, degenerated people. We are compelled to spend literally billions and billions of dollars a year in both private and public drains on our resources to provide the doctors, the nurses, the hospitals to correct the endless illnesses caused by obesity and overeating.

I have been a critic of waste in defense. But I am certain that America has wasted far more of its substance, many, many times more, at the dinner table than it has even in the appalling extravagance of the Pentagon. I believe that we as a people have been enfeebled more by the single bad habit of a surfeit of food than by any other.

Plan Your Weight Battle

The determination which we discussed in the exercise sections of this book, when you decide that you're going to walk those four miles or run those three or four miles or swim the nine hundred yards, applies with the same force to your decision to diet.

If your diet is going to be a success, it's very important that you make a conscious and deliberate decision and then write it down as a genuine resolution. Next you have to announce it to your husband or wife, your children, your friends, your fellow workers, so that *everybody* knows it. Make it just as hard to break your resolution as possible. Determine that you're going to keep it.

I suppose all of us have made decisions we have failed to

keep for more than a day or two or maybe even more than a few minutes. The difference between being free to exercise an effective will and being a slave to your appetite goes to the depth and strength of your loyalty, to the commitment you make when you say yes I'm going to diet or yes, I'm going to run, or yes, I'm going to walk, or yes, I'm going to swim.

The Four Essential Steps

If you're really going to give yourself a chance to keep the decision you make, here are some suggestions I think you'll find very useful. In fact, I find them essential:

1. In the first place, make sure you think about your resolution to diet very carefully. Spend some time reflecting about it, about all its implications, the sacrifices it means; about why you are doing it and what you have to gain.

2. Second, and most important of all, make your resolution realistic. Make it a resolution that you know in your heart you can and will keep. Make it moderate.

A good way to do this is to look honestly at your eating habits. Keep a record of what you eat—include *everything*—for a day or two before you start dieting. Then decide what you can cut out most easily, without really missing it.

For instance, it may be that you simply want to cut out that second cocktail, that second helping of food or bread and butter or rich dessert. Make it just that simple, just that limited for a while. It may be that you won't lose very much weight this way, but you'll find out what you can do and you'll have the great pleasure of developing confidence in your resolution: you can indeed keep the pledge you make to yourself.

3. Third, when you make your commitment about what you're going to do on your diet, make it for a long enough period so that it will do a job.

Obviously you won't lose more than a fraction of a pound if you just give up a little food for only a few days. You might set the goal of staying on your diet for a month, maybe two months. You might try to stay on your diet until you reach a certain weight. Choose a goal that will make a difference but don't make it too ambitious. It's very important to be realistic or you'll get discouraged.

Once you have decided what you're going to cut out, do not—*do not*—become more ambitious until you have fully completed the time period you chose originally.

When you make a commitment to diet for a month, set a definite time for review of your commitment in which you reconsider how well you've done.

That might be after one week, then after two weeks, then after three weeks. Consider how well you've kept it, reflect on the times when you've been tempted to break it, and use your imagination as much as you can to determine what you can do to eliminate the temptations or distract yourself from them so that you won't be as tempted in the future.

For example, you could keep one calorie counter in your kitchen and one in your briefcase or handbag, to reinforce your determination to use your calorie counter faithfully so you're sure you know just how many calories you have been consuming. At least use one on a regular spot-check basis.

4. If you're going to make this resolution to diet successful, you should do it based on the best advice you can get from your doctor, a good dietician, if you know one, or your own common sense about the importance of continuing to have a balanced diet with sufficient proteins, carbohydrates, fats, and vitamins and minerals so that your system will remain healthy.

After you have the best advice you can get, and you have considered it carefully, make up your own mind; don't let anybody else make it up for you. This should be your resolution, not your doctor's, your mother's, your father's, your son's, your daughter's, your friends', or anyone else's. If it's your very own resolution, made by you but announced just as widely as you can bring yourself to do, it is one you are much more likely to keep than if it is imposed on you from without.

Then you are doing what this book is really all about. You are achieving the freedom to make up your own mind and determine your own fate by self-discipline.

23 · Your Best Diet Tactics

ABOUT TWENTY YEARS AGO Dr. Norman Jolliffe, a specialist in nutrition, developed the concept of the "appestat." Appestat is the term Dr. Jolliffe used to describe the appetite-regulating mechanism that tells us when we've eaten enough.

Dr. Jolliffe found that the appestat is virtually universal in children and young people. Unless they are urged or forced to eat too much, children and young people tend to eat the amount they need for energy and growth. They are lean and full of vitality and bounce. According to Dr. Jolliffe, various factors can cause this appestat to become weaker as we get older. We begin to overeat because our families overeat or for a variety of emotional reasons, and after a short time overeating seems normal. Our appestat is no longer functioning.

If everyone's appestat were still working, this chapter would be unnecessary. In a sense, this whole section on diet is an attempt to provide those who have lost their appestats with a moral or mental equivalent.

I've found it very helpful to recognize and face squarely the fact that as I've gotten older, my appestat has vanished. When I was younger it was impossible for me to sit down and eat an eight-ounce steak, a baked potato, a generous helping of fresh peas, a large salad, and a dessert of mixed fruit without feeling so full that I couldn't eat another bite if I were forced to do so.

This is no longer true.

I Can Eat and Eat and Eat

Now I could sit down and eat just what I have described and eat another meal and a third meal on top of it without feeling that I'd eaten too much. After the first meal the food wouldn't taste as good, but my system could absorb it. There would be no warning or signal to tell me to stop. I could go on and on and eat two or three times as much as my body needs.

You too may find that your appestat, which may have served you well in your earlier days, has faded as you got older. It means that you need a substitute or several substitutes—a calorie counter, a scale, a mirror, a pinch test, and all the other hints and suggestions of this chapter.

Here are the best friends your good health can have. These are your tools for keeping your weight down.

Calorie Counter

1. Get yourself a calorie counter. You can get it from the Department of Agriculture or from almost any bookstore; even newsstands may have them. It is a little pamphlet that tells you precisely how many calories there are in every kind of food you eat.

Get your calorie counter and use it. The next time you sit down to a meal, any meal, count up your calories. If you are male, adult, weigh 150 pounds and are about as active as most people, you can just about sustain your weight at 2,500 calories a day. That means three meals at 700 calories each and a 400-calorie snack. But you must count everything, and I mean everything. If you have a beer or a highball, count that. If you have a soft drink count that. If you have a candy bar count that; it will add up. Even if you have a stick of gum, believe it or not there are 10 calories in a stick of gum—count that. Nutritionists have determined that there are about 3,500 calories in a pound. In other words, if over a week you reduce your caloric consumption 3,500 calories below what it takes to sustain your weight, you will lose one pound in that week. Fortunately, 3,500 is a very convenient number of calories per week, because there are seven days in a week. Divide 7 into 3,500 and you'll find that if you cut the 2,500 calories you need to sustain your weight down to 2,000 calories a day and maintain the same amount of physical activity, you will lose a pound in that week.

As we said in the exercise section, it's no trick at all to take off that same pound without reducing your caloric intake one iota, provided you step up your consumption of calories by more physical activity. If you burn an additional 500 calories a day for a week by prolonged exercise, and if you do not increase your food consumption during that week, then you will also lose a pound. You have that option. Of course if you reduce your caloric consumption from 2,500 calories to 2,000 calories *and* step up your physical activity, so that your system consumes an additional 500 calories a day for the whole week, you will take off not one pound but two pounds, one because of your diet and a second because of your exercise.

Another, absolutely essential method of reinforcing your will is to force yourself to use the calorie counter just as much as possible. There will come a time when you know how many calories there are in each kind of food you eat. As a matter of fact, it will be only a few days until you're able to estimate your calories precisely. But make sure you do that, and at first don't hesitate to write down what the calories are in each meal, each snack, and everything you put in your mouth. You'll find that this too will be a great reinforcer in holding down your caloric content. It's one thing to smear an extra pat of butter on your bread when you don't estimate the calories. But when you realize that that extra amount is 100 fat calories for a tablespoon of butter and you understand it, and you understand that it means you have to deprive yourself of eating a far more filling, tempting, and delicious apple, pear, or orange—which add up to about the same as that big pat of butter—it's a lot easier to pass up the butter.

When you concentrate on losing weight, especially without changing physical activity, your calorie counter is a dear friend.

Scales

2. A second dear friend, and sometimes even dearer and more necessary, is your scale. Get a bathroom scale, test it and be sure that it is reasonably accurate, then make friends with it by weighing yourself every single day at precisely the same time under precisely the same circumstances.

I find it psychologically advantageous to weigh myself when I weigh the least possible amount—after I have slept all night, done my calisthenics, run five miles to the office, and had a shower and a rubdown. At that point, before I have breakfast, I weigh myself.

If I weigh myself after breakfast I weigh more. If I weigh myself without that run I weigh more. If I weigh myself after a five-mile run in the summer, when it's very warm, and I have perspired off two or three pounds, I weigh less than on cooler mornings. These are just details. By and large, if you weigh yourself at the same time every day, under the same circumstances, you will be able to keep an accurate and honest record of your progress or lack of it.

Losing weight and keeping it off is after all a matter of being honest with yourself. Squarely face the fact that you have gained or that you have not lost enough. Recognizing the truth is your first big step. It is very reassuring to watch your weight go down, and your scale can be a real buddy when it says to you, Billy, my boy, you're a real hero. You lost a pound today or this week. And it is a mighty useful critic when it says, Billy, you did it again. You can't get away with it. You ate too much last night and here's the result—right here.

Once you get your weight down—and as I say, this is the easiest part of dieting—keep it down by using your scale in something like the following way. This is the way I do it and it may be helpful to you.

If I weigh even half a pound more than my target weight, I go on a diet for that day. It's a modest, limited diet that consists of skipping the toast and butter I usually have for breakfast, not having soup with lunch, and, depending on how far over my target I am, perhaps skipping the apple I usually have in the afternoon and holding the snack at night to just one piece of fruit.

That may not seem like much but I have found that it almost always brings me back to the desired weight. If it doesn't, I simply stay on the diet for two days.

This exactness lets me freely give in on occasion to eating an extra amount of delicious food or having a rare bout with a hot-fudge sundae, peanut butter and crackers, or some other favorite. When I do this I know that I will have to pay the price and pay it promptly. That daily scale and the immediate reaction to it are a sure and certain way of preventing yourself from being a yo-yo. You won't bounce way up as you bounced down. You determine surely and firmly in advance just what your goal is going to be. If you know you're going to get down to 150 pounds or 110 pounds, you can stay with it.

It's a matter of not postponing—not even for one day— weight loss whenever you find that you are over the weight you want to maintain. The regular discipline of losing weight instantly, the same day you find out you have added it, is an enormous help in reinforcing your determination to eat moderately. It will become almost second nature to you to say no when you realize that those extra calories are going to have to be paid for the very next day.

Some heart specialists argue that it is the gaining of weight that aggravates the heart disease rather than obesity itself. If you succeed in getting your weight down by fifteen or twenty pounds and go back up again, you may have done more harm than good. The way to avoid that is to make it clear and emphatic that you are going to stay down at your target weight come hell or high water.

I'm virtually certain that without my friendly scale I might have taken off the weight I did but I could never have kept it off as I determined I would.

Tape Measure

You may want to supplement and reinforce your weight losing by having a tape measure handy and measuring your waist once a month to see what kind of progress you're making. If you are combining exercise with diet, this may be especially reassuring. It's just as important to transfer that fat into muscle as it is to lose weight—maybe even more important, depending on your condition. It's really astonishing what a combination of vigorous, prolonged, regular exercise and a persistent program of holding down calories can do for reducing that waist.

Signs in Kitchen

A little device that I've found very useful is to put a sign up in the kitchen, where my will power has collapsed in the past.

For example, for months I was putting on weight simply by eating cookies. I couldn't resist them; the cooky jar was something I couldn't stay away from. My children are very tolerant and gentle with me, and think I'm a little too hard on myself. They enjoy cookies and there is no reason we shouldn't have them around. I finally found one way I could stay out of the cooky jar—and it broke my bad habit completely. I simply put a sign on the jar saying, DAD, KEEP OUT. I put that sign up more than a year ago and I've not eaten a cooky since. The kids enjoyed teasing me about it, which was exactly what I wanted and it really worked. You might try that. Put a little sign up with your name on it: Joe, Jim, Jack, Jean, Jane—Stay Away—Keep Out! As a matter of fact, it wouldn't be a bad idea to put it on your jar of peanut butter or even on your refrigerator, if you want to eliminate those nighttime snacks that are destroying your will to diet.

Brag a Little

It's a good idea to put every psychological force you can summon on your side when you start taking off weight. Don't hide it; let your friends, neighbors, office associates, those who work with you at the plant know that you're dieting. Talk about it. Tell them what you're trying to do. Tell them what progress you're making. Tell them how much you weigh.

Of course it's easy to become a bore this way, but if you just mention it once in a while most people are interested and will encourage you. It will help you a great deal if others take that interest and realize what you're trying to do and what kind of progress you're making.

Being open about your problem and discussing it is one of the principles behind Alcoholics Anonymous and such organizations as TOPS (Take Off Pounds Sensibly), and Weight Watchers. People who have the same problem get together, work with each other, help each other, comment on the progress they've made, and applaud each other's successes. If you are the kind of person—and almost all of us are—who responds to social encouragement and pressure, this is a great way to be sure that you will take weight off.

It may be that you won't find it convenient to join a Weight Watchers or TOPS group. If you can't, you can create a good deal of the same kind of helpful psychology simply by telling your friends about your aims and organizing their psychological influence to help you.

Mirror

Speaking of psychological boosters, don't overlook your mirror. In the privacy of home there is no reason why you can't strip in front of your bathroom mirror, or your full-length mirror if you have one in your bedroom. Try to get a mirror big enough so that you can see most of your body, then strip and notice the kind of progress you've been able to make. Taking off weight can really make you feel proud, and properly so. You can see it.

It's also a good idea to reinforce your determination to lose weight by looking at yourself in the mirror and admitting how ugly the fat is. Remind yourself too that it will shorten your life and make what years you have left miserable if you don't get rid of it and keep it off. Just imagine how you look to others in a bathing suit and how much better you'll look if you take the weight off. And as you take it off, look in that mirror every morning just the way you step on the scale every day. Be honest with yourself. See whether your body—stomach, hips, legs, chest, and arms—is as lean as it should be. The mirror can be another real friend.

Pinch Test

For a more precise measure, and a very good one, there is the pinch test. You can take the pinch test on several parts of your body. Pinch a fold of flesh on your side, about halfway between your hip and your underarm. If that pinch is less than half an inch, then your weight isn't bad. If it's more than half an inch you are a Mr. or Ms. Flab and it's time you did something about it.

For a sterner test, pinch the flesh on your stomach.

Dr. Lawrence Lamb, the heart specialist and syndicated health columnist, contends that the skin on your body ought to be like that on the back of your hand, lean and thin and firm. Not one adult American in five hundred can meet that kind of test, but that's a goal to shoot at, and believe me, you can come a great deal closer to it than you are now. After you've taken the weight off, making that test regularly can remind you and help you in your determination.

Time Your Exercise

In this section I won't speak much about the value of prolonged exercise for taking off weight, but I would emphasize that if you read the exercise sections of this book and follow them, you can be helped greatly to say NO to that tempting food. One secret is to time your exercise so that much of it comes before your big meal.

I find, for example, that vigorously walking the five miles back from my office just before dinnertime greatly reduces my appetite. This may be hard for most people to believe because they think of exercise as creating appetite. What prolonged exercise does is depress hunger pangs. You aren't as hungry because the digestive system that normally is at work demanding food is at work during your exercise providing the circulation, the blood production and consumption, that your system needs to keep exercising.

Water

Here is another little trick that helps you keep your weight off and your appetite down just before dinner. If you walk very vigorously, or jog, or run a distance, normally your desire will be for water rather than food. You'll be dehydrated and you'll want to drink something. You could drink a high-calorie soda or fruit juice, but that would be the worst thing you could do.

Instead, drink water. I can tell you that nothing in the world tastes better than cold water when you're thirsty after a long period of vigorous exercise. Drink the water slowly but drink as much of it as you want—a glass, two glasses, three glasses. Then you will find your appetite very substantially diminished.

As a matter of fact, it's a fine idea to drink a good deal of water throughout the day. It's a great help in taking off weight for several reasons. For one thing, water is filling. For another, it has no caloric value whatsoever. All of us drink beverages that have some kind of caloric content. We put sugar in our coffee or tea, we drink fruit juices, alcoholic beverages, or beer or dairy products. All of them have their place, but all of them also have caloric content and some have a great number of calories. Your thirst can be slaked much more readily by water, with its caloric content of *zero*.

Smaller Portions

I used to prepare a large steak or a large piece of fish for dinner until I started checking my friendly calorie counter and found that a three-ounce steak provided far more calories than I realized and was sufficient for a substantial dinner. A 4-ounce serving of fish can be delicious and filling, ample if you eat it slowly. Many vegetables have such a low caloric content that you can have a large, filling portion. At any rate, keep the servings of all foods you eat within the limit your calorie counter dictates. And when your appetite is reasonably satisfied, get up, leave the table, leave the kitchen, get out of the way of temptation.

Ignore Your Jealous Friends

Much of what you've read so far argues that if you follow my prescription on exercise, diet, and rest you're going to be better-looking. This is often a matter of opinion.

You may be healthier and feel better, but in the eyes of many of your friends you may not look as good as you did.

In my judgment this is one of the biggest pitfalls in getting to the right weight. A great majority of people associate leanness with ill health. And it's true that if you lose a great deal of weight and you're over forty or fifty, your face is likely to wrinkle temporarily and the circles to deepen under your eyes, making you look tired at least for a while.

I know because this is exactly what's happened to me. I do look better if I weigh 158 pounds, but I don't feel as well. I don't have the stamina and I know I'm not as healthy.

Ego being what it is, pride in looking well being what it is, I'm sure that the you-look-thin attitude of our friends is a major obstacle to getting our weight down to a really low and healthy level. It's one reason for so many yo-yos. If a yo-yo's wife or a woman at the office or the guy who works right next to him at the machine shop tells him that he looks so skinny a good wind will blow him away, while his appetite is urging him to give in and enjoy life, that's all he needs to push him over the edge.

After I had gotten my weight down to 143, my colleagues in the Senate began telling me I looked too thin. Often people spoke to me in a tone of concern or apprehension, as though they were consoling a man with a dire illness. There was no denying that my weight loss had made me look older, and I decided to consult an authority to find out what I could do about it. I wrote to Dr. Lawrence Lamb, the eminent heart specialist and author of a syndicated column on heart disease and related problems. He suggested isometric-type facial exercises and these really do help a great deal. Also, they're easy to do.

Hair Transplants

Having found the facial exercises beneficial, I decided that I would look even better and younger if I had more hair. After reading about the success of hair transplant operations, I decided to go ahead, and I am delighted with the results. It was an expensive and painful process, but very worthwhile. Of course a decision of this kind is a very personal one—I had been bald for almost fifteen years, so it was very exciting to have hair again.

Flee Temptation

When you watch television or sit around talking with your friends during the evening, be sure there is no tempting snack put out or available for you to munch on. Beer, buttered popcorn, peanuts, and candy play complete havoc with your calorie consumption program.

What I have found necessary in order to take off and keep off weight is to throw out some of the foods I especially like. Peanut butter, for instance, is something I dream about, and peanut butter and crackers is a snack that I simply cannot resist. I finally had to take my last two jars of peanut butter and put them in the garbage, saying a sad farewell to them along with a large box of beautiful crisp crackers, and it'll be a long, long time before I buy peanut butter and crackers again. While they were there they were my friendly enemies. If you have a tasty, tempting, tantalizing snack stashed away, get rid of it. Don't hesitate to throw it out.

President Harry Truman had a statement which has been used many, many times by politicians who are criticized and denounced. Harry used to say, "If you can't stand the heat, get out of the kitchen." The President meant, If you can't stand criticism, get out of politics. Because most of us can't stand the exposure to food without getting into it, we should get out of that kitchen.

If you're a housewife who has to prepare food for your children and your husband day after day, this is the kind of advice you can't possibly take. Under those circumstances you have to do your best to be a nondrinking bartender. You have to make a rule that as long as you are preparing food you can't touch it. There's one place and only one place where you eat, and that's at the dining-room table. You don't snack or taste food except your own food at your own place. It's expecting an awful lot of any human being, but that's the price you have to pay if you're going to hold down your weight.

Recognize: Hunger Is Good for You

There is another psychological problem in dieting. Many of us have been so conditioned to eat, and eat regularly and eat a great deal, that we feel that if we cut down or even eliminate a meal the effect could be disastrous to our health, or if not disastrous seriously negative. We seem to have forgotten that people have fasted for a day at a time and often longer without damage to their health. So make friends, good warm friends, with the feeling of being hungry.

Take some time to really think about that hungry feeling the next time it comes. Most of us just automatically reach for something to eat and eat it. If you think seriously about that hunger feeling, it is not bad, especially when you think about what it's doing for you. Because it's when you're hungry that you know your system is calling out for food, which means the fat in your body is beginning to be burned. It means the fat is melting from your waist. You're on the road to a healthier future with less illness.

Think about hunger. Dwell on it. This should reinforce your will. I find it develops my moral muscle.

You may want to go one step further. Try this: Develop hunger. Eat less or even skip a meal. Familiarize yourself carefully and thoughtfully with that hunger feeling. Notice what it does for your taste buds. Notice how much more enthusiastic you are when you look forward to your next meal. Consider how much better that meal will taste because you have become hungry. This doesn't mean you must gorge because you've become hungry—that would destroy all the value and benefit of having forgone food to develop the hunger. It does mean that when you eat you will enjoy it more. The pleasure will be intensified. Your taste buds will do much more for you.

The most artful, professional, accomplished cooking in the world, the most loving preparation of the food that you enjoy the most, won't do as much for your genuine enjoyment as being really hungry.

When you eat when you're hungry, eat slowly and eat self-consciously. Concentrate on the whole process. Stop long enough to notice whether or not your hunger pangs are being satisfied. When they are, consider slowing down and stopping. That isn't easy when the food is still available and tasty. But believe me, it's the clue, the first big step to getting your weight under control.

I find that even though I know better, I will justify the consumption of more food than I need or should eat on the grounds that the food I'm eating is good for me. Almost any food, no matter how perfect it is or how good it is for you, is very bad indeed in excess.

Experiment a Little

The trick I have developed to overcome all these psychological hangups about how you have to keep eating if you're going to keep healthy is to experiment a little. I have experimented not only with a cutdown of food, but also with a complete absence of food. Fasting (see Chapter 24) was an eye-opener for me.

If fasting for a whole day seems too much for you, you can overcome a lot of your hangups about the necessity for eating by simply skipping the meal you like the most. All of us skip breakfast once in a while, or lunch, but most of us look forward enthusiastically and eagerly to dinner at night and snacks after dinner. Try this tomorrow: Eat a light breakfast and a light lunch, no snacks or drinks in the afternoon, and at night skip dinner entirely. You'll be surprised how swiftly the hunger pangs go away, especially if you stay out of the kitchen and away from the dinner table.

At first skipping dinner may seem unsociable to your husband or wife or to your kids, but if you explain they'll understand. You can spend that much more time reading, exercising, watching TV, or practicing relaxation, and if you're normal and healthy and not underweight, you'll find that you have absolutely no adverse effects and perhaps some positive and enjoyable good side effects. You might also try fasting for just twenty-four hours. But more of that when we get to the next chapter.

Of course the key to saying NO to food is to develop real motivation that will stay with you and persuade you that it's worth following a day-by-day diet of moderation.

24 · Fasting, but Only Under Medical Supervision

SHE WAS FIVE FEET TALL and weighed a good, solid three hundred pounds. She grunted and groaned up the stairs, the four steps to the doctor's office. She entered the waiting room and sat with a crushing gasp of relief, filling an oversize chair. In a few minutes the secretary ushered her into the doctor's office. The doctor told her to sit down, looked at her, looked away, and said, "You have thirty days to live."

She gasped and whitened. "That's giving it to me pretty straight, ain't it, Doc?"

"That's giving it to you honestly," he replied, "you're going to be dead in thirty days."

"Doc, is there anything I can do?"

He said, "Yes, there's just one thing you can do. For the next month you eat nothing. Drink water, all the water you want, but you drink nothing else and you eat absolutely nothing at all. And I want to tell you, if you eat anything, and I mean anything, you're going to die."

The woman wiped the perspiration from her forehead, groaned, and as she left the doctor's office he shook his head.

Thirty days later she came back, singing, happy, relaxed, and said, "Doc, that's the best thing that ever happened to me. I didn't eat a thing. I'm doing my own laundry for the first time. I was able to cook for my husband without even tasting anything. I'm going to make it!"

The doctor was my father. This happened many, many years ago, but that's a true story. The fat lady wasn't the first person to be enormously benefited by simply going without food entirely for a prolonged period of time.

No, I don't suggest that you go out today and eat nothing for the next thirty days. You should never fast without being under the direct supervision of your doctor, with his full knowledge and approval and precisely the way he suggests it. But it's worth considering.

My father told me about one woman who had suffered from arthritis for many years. She went on a thirty-six-day fast, drank nothing but water, and found that for the first time in years she could move hands, legs, and arms easily and without pain.

That doesn't mean that fasting is a cure for arthritis. Starvation happened to be just right for this particular woman and it might not be right for the next hundred people who tried it. But there is an element in fasting which is useful and makes sense for everyone. There is no question that many of us slowly and gradually poison ourselves by not only eating too much but eating foods that accumulate weakening and enfeebling fat.

There are institutions which people enter to fast under supervision. In many cases, the faster will benefit, and benefit more than he has with any other kind of therapy.

Try a Short, Very Short Fast

I'm not suggesting a thirty-day fast or even a ten-day fast. I'm suggesting something else. I'm suggesting that to get an understanding of your system and how to control your consumption of food, skip a meal, even skip eating for an entire twenty-four hours. But by all means do not do more than this without, as I say, consultation with your doctor. Chances are he would warn you against going any further than a day or two.

If you skip a meal, it should be your big meal of the day.

If like most of us you eat more at dinner, have a light breakfast, a light lunch, and then nothing until you eat a light breakfast the next day.

I did this for the first time in my life not long ago, and I found that the effect was nothing like what I had expected. Of course I was hungry at mealtime and for an hour or so afterward, but not very hungry, and the hunger soon disappeared. I slept well that night. I wasn't hungrier than usual the following day, and before breakfast I was able to run five miles and swim thirty-six lengths of the pool (nine hundred yards) without any diminution in strength. I had no headache, no stomach-ache, and none of the other difficulties I had expected. A little later I skipped an entire day—a full twenty-four hours without eating. Once again I found no diminution at all in strength or in the way I felt.

I've read as you may have about the importance of maintaining a certain level of blood sugar. Obviously, if you don't eat at all for a full day the level of blood sugar simply has to drop. But if you are reasonably strong and healthy, one day may have no significant effect on the way you feel. On the other hand, it may make you feel tired or weak. If it does, not even a one-meal fast would be wise. In that case, cut down, but don't cut out without a doctor's okay.

Advantages of a Short Fast

And the weight loss can really be dramatic. When I gave up food for a full twenty-four hours the weight loss was literally ten pounds. That's a very deceptive weight loss, because you can only lose a pound for every 3,500 calories that you do not eat and that your body uses up. Any assumption that even with my vigorous exercise I use as much as 3,500 calories may be an optimistic assumption. My natural weight loss was probably a maximum of a pound. The rest— the other nine of the ten-pound drop in weight—was the loss of water, a loss that was restored over the next few days.

Fasting probably does have a significant cleansing effect on the body. It also has a resting effect, because the digestive system doesn't have to work. There is nothing to digest. But what I want to emphasize here is that fasting can be a helpful tool for losing weight and controlling weight.

Once you realize that you're not going to be very hungry if you give up food, and once you realize that you can lose half a pound or a pound a day by doing so, you will realize how arithmetically comforting is the relationship between the reduction in your food consumption and your loss of weight.

Fasting is so subject to abuse and can be so seriously harmful to your whole system that it is not the ideal way to lose weight, and of course it's an impossible way to control weight.

But once you understand how much you can lose by giving food up, it should be easier (it certainly is for me) to simply eat less.

Fasting Teaches a Lesson

If you lose no physical efficiency, no mental alertness by eating nothing for twenty-four hours, you can hardly justify the rationalizations that I find myself tempted to accept when I want to eat and know I shouldn't: Eating will keep up my blood sugar, I say, will help me retain my alertness and stay awake. I remember asking one very heavy friend why he didn't try to cut down on his consumption. He told me, "Because I have headaches."

I'm just positive this was nonsense. I'm sure he had the headaches but that they were brought on by his expectation that he must have headaches if he didn't eat. I'm sure that if he tried fasting he would have a more constructive attitude toward losing weight and keeping his weight down.

Don't overlook the genuine benefits of fasting. Once again, if you're going to do it, by all means do it with the advice of your doctor.

Once you have fasted, you will understand far better how easy it is for your body to remain healthy and strong and to accept less food. If you, like me, have gone through a good part of your life without missing a meal for an entire day, "Try it, you'll like it."

25 · I Disagree—a Little—with Weight Watchers

MY OWN APPROACH to losing weight and then maintaining a low weight is quite contrary to at least some of the professional, commercial weight-losing and controlling advocates.

There is at least one group that believes both daily use of scales and reliance on calorie counters can be pernicious. They give all kinds of complicated psychological explanations.

To me their arguments just don't add up at all.

The number-one principle in losing weight is that you develop the courage to look squarely at the facts. Fact one is that extra calories put on weight. Unless you utilize all the calories you consume, you are inevitably going to gain weight. This is something you must constantly keep in mind, and the calorie counter and the scale are the two best ways to do it.

Everything you put into your mouth and swallow, except water, has a caloric value. To me it is a highly useful deterrent to realize the very high caloric content of, say, one pat of butter. I'm far less likely to indulge in additional ice cream when I know that every spoonful adds almost 50 calories, and that every tablespoon of my favorite peanut butter adds 100 calories.

And as for scales, there is just no possible way I could get myself down to my ideal goal of 143 pounds without weighing myself every day at exactly the same time and under the same circumstances. Sure, there are erratic weight losses from day to day. But you get so you very quickly understand why.

Fortunately, I find that when I eat more than I should, the scale tends to exaggerate the pickup of that particular day's overeating by a pound or two. I have found that if I eat an additional 1,000 calories my weight goes up one and a half pounds the next day. That weight gain is largely temporary, but it's a good, quick reminder.

Nevertheless, you can't be dogmatic about such things. Some people become confused with calorie counters—the arithmetic of it is too much. Or somehow they can't summon up the maturity or psychological strength to resist eating ice cream, candy, and butter and will eat these fattening foods in preference to more nutritious fruit and vegetables just because they like the taste. Then they will calculate how they can get away with simply taking their caloric allowance in less nutritious but tastier foods.

For the Psychologically Mature

But if you have any psychological maturity, which is just plain intelligence, you realize that only a very little butter, ice cream, candy, or cookies uses up your limited caloric allowance. Your appetite is far from satisfied; the food you have eaten is dead, with little or no real nutritional value and few vitamins. You lose your vitality and become far more prone to disease.

Relying on your caloric counter, you are facing the truth constantly and objectively. You *know* just exactly what you are putting into your system with *every* mouthful you swallow.

Now let's be fair about this. There is no reason to be confused when you use the calorie counter, provided you stay with it for a few days. Because it takes only a few **days** to develop a quick and easy understanding of precisely the number of calories in virtually all the foods you consume.

Second, there's nothing more simple, clear, or truthful than the mathematical precision of that scale. When you get on the scale and you know you've gained, you know you're a loser. When you've lost or maintained your weight, if that's your goal, you're a winner. You have faced the truth. You have the truth each day.

The commercial weight-loser people who warn you against scales and calorie counters have to have a substitute.

Self-Control

After all, if *you don't know* just how much you are adding to your system when you eat, and if you don't know whether you have won or lost every day, you, yourself, can't be in control of your own fate. You aren't the one who is going to determine whether you lose the weight you want to lose or maintain your weight at the goal you choose. You must relate to others.

That doesn't mean that you're a lost soul or that you can't win. It means you must rely on the aids and devices the commercial organization suggest, and they can be very helpful indeed. Weight Watchers, for example, has a record of success with many people.

The unique difference as far as I am concerned is that with the Proxmire approach you rely on yourself. You are self-reliant, self-disciplined. And self-reliance and self-discipline are the price of freedom. That is the simple and direct message of this book.

There are many people who simply don't want to be self-reliant or self-disciplined. They would prefer to lean on others. And there's nothing wrong with that. It just means that you're a different kind of a person.

Try Both

I suggest that you might try both approaches. You might join a group and rely on it to keep up your morale; rely on it to suggest your menus and to indicate the foods you can or cannot eat. Relying on them for guidance and support and direction may work.

Certainly if you want a comprehensive program of physical fitness, including not only systematic and effective weight control but systematic and effective exercise and systematic and effective relaxation, you simply have to become self-reliant. It's too much to expect to join a group that will enable you to do all these things unless you can find or create an incredibly totalitarian society that will organize every phase of your life.

26 · The Vitamin Battle

YES, I TAKE VITAMINS every day, a number of different ones. But I should make several things about vitamins clear at the very beginning of this chapter. First, the case for them is tentative. A large proportion of the medical profession and many of the best qualified nutrition specialists in government service and in the universities challenge the usefulness of vitamin pills.

The argument goes like this: Those who oppose the purchase and consumption of vitamin tablets and capsules say that for the normal healthy adult with a well-balanced diet, additional vitamins are unnecessary. A balanced diet with milk, meat, fruit, vegetables, and bread-cereal will give all that is required of vitamins, minerals, and other nutrients.

Right, But!

They may be right. They probably are. But that's not the end of it. Consider the qualifications. First, "for the normal, healthy adult" undoubtedly leaves out millions of Americans, including many adults. How many are normal? For example, I'm healthy and strong, and feel great, but I have an abnormally low hemoglobin count. A capsule supplement has been useful in getting my hemoglobin count within the normal range. We have some of the best doctors in the world taking care of senators, and they tell me my diet is just about perfect, but it's not good enough to give me the hemoglobin-building substance my health demands.

So number one, in my view, is that literally tens of millions of Americans—very possibly a majority—have some physiological deficiency, usually minor (like mine) but still definite, that can be helped by supplementary vitamins.

Second, the antivitamin-pill people make a gigantic and demonstrably erroneous assumption when they imply that most Americans have adequate and balanced diets. Every study indicates exactly the contrary. Millions of Americans, including many with high incomes, have miserably unbalanced diets. The studies show that the typical American diet is far too high in commercial sugar, and in bread, pastry, and an infinite variety of snacks with the nutritional value milled out.

Now I would agree that the prime objective of nutritionists should be to get the American people on to the right diet and keep them there. But how unrealistic can you get? You and I know that as long as it is cheaper to manufacture breakfast foods and breads and sweets of all kinds that can be sold for far more than their cost and preserved indefinitely in all their dead, empty content, and as long as these food manufacturers are free to buy endless time on television and in other advertising media, millions of Americans are going to persist in stuffing their bodies with food that lacks the vitamins they ought to have.

The Long Run Is Far Away

And even beyond that, the human animal is not always or even usually motivated by what is good for him in the long run. Go into any lunch counter or restaurant patronized by teenagers and see what they order. For years the favorite was a cola drink and French fries smothered in ketchup. Most youngsters suck on soft drinks or candy bars or popsicles. These foods have almost no nutritional value. They provide sugar, caffeine (in the case of some colas). They make you fat. They kill the appetite for other foods.

You give me a nickel for each child you see with one of these, and I'll give you a dollar for every child you can show me eating an apple, an orange, a carrot stick, or any other food that has natural vitamins in it. You make that exchange with me and I'll have most of what's in your wallet by the end of the day, any day you want to go with me, anywhere in any city where children and teenagers congregate.

A prime necessity is to recognize that the penalty we pay for an inadequate diet does not come due for years—usually many years.

That ten-year-old who never eats an orange and drinks soft drinks at his meals instead of milk may not suffer from it for thirty or forty years. Walk down the street today and observe people over fifty. Most of them are in various pathetic stages of disability: pallid, weak, obese, moving painfully and slowly.

Now maybe these people are happy human beings leading a good life. Some of them undoubtedly are. The mind and spirit can and occasionally does triumph over a broken body. We think of Elizabeth Barrett Browning, Franklin Roosevelt, Robert Louis Stevenson, and many other people. You and I know some of them personally. But for every person whose indomitable or loving spirit shines through the pain and misery of disease, there are ten or more who are just plain miserable human beings.

What's Wrong with Health?

All right, forget the numbers game. Maybe all or most of these people are happy in spite of their pathetic bodies. Can you doubt that if this is the case they would be much, very much happier if they were healthy? The total amount of human misery caused by too much refined sugar and too little fruit, too many pies and cakes and too little cottage cheese and skim milk, or too little in the way of vitamin supplements if their diet was poor, is a problem to stagger the mind.

Wasteful Government Spending on Health

As a United States Senator concerned with run-away government spending, I should remind you that it staggers your pocketbook too. For years I have led the fight in the Senate against senseless waste in military spending, weapons systems that cost billions more than they should, space extravaganzas that drain the public trough for little useful public purpose. These wastes are appalling and I intend to continue to fight them as long as I remain in the United States Senate.

But the waste in Medicare and the waste of any new, more comprehensive health care is going to be even more appalling and it will hit your pocketbook even harder.

I'm convinced that most of the immense cost of Medicare is because Ameicans have become too soft, too fat, too lazy, too self-indulgent, and far too careless about what they eat.

Vitamins and Special Physical Problems

Many books tell you what vitamins to take to overcome various physiological problems. I won't do that because I feel very strongly that this should be done on the advice of your physician after he examines you thoroughly.

Please, please have this kind of examination. Ask your physician to suggest a diet. That doesn't mean you can't eat everything you like in moderation. It means that some things you should eat regularly—in moderation, but regularly. Then your doctor may or may not suggest vitamin supplements.

Do this and you will be taking a big step toward getting yourself off the taxpayers' back when you reach middle age and beyond. You will not have to worry as much about the prospect of becoming a burden on your children or a miserable physical hulk that, at best, must smile through your tears of physical agony.

Increase Your Odds

Not diet, not exercise, not relaxation—not all of them faithfully and constantly followed throughout a lifetime—can guarantee a healthy middle or old age, but your odds will greatly increase.

Jimmy the Greek might handicap you at five-to-one to become a shambling, muttering wreck if you live into your seventies and eighties without exercise and adequate diet and no attention to your tensions. He'd have to lower the odds to something like one-to-five—in other words, overwhelmingly—for a good life if you follow the discipline suggested here.

One other note, but an important one. I said at the outset of this chapter that I take a number of vitamins. I do, just to be on the safe side. But I am very careful to take a small, limited amount of each. I never exceed the dosage suggested. Certainly some vitamins taken excessively can be harmful. A limited amount, even if your diet is good, can't hurt, and it may enable you to hedge your bets in case the preponderant medical opinion of today turns out to be wrong.

VII· RELAXATION

27 · Why Relax?

To MANY OF US the whole world seems to be living at the top of its voice. The superamplified rock band clashes out our new "noise" culture. Cars hurtle along our highways faster than ever. Horns and jet planes and pneumatic drills shout at us. Radio and television blare into our ears. You and I strain to beat the other guy in school, in sports, in politics, or just at the next stop light.

The world may be better or worse. Who knows? We do know that it's louder and tenser than ever, and that more and more of our people hate it. They hate it so much they're giving up. They're surrendering and saying "uncle" with drugs and booze, with suicide and breakdowns.

Again and again we are told that the tension, the pressure of modern life is just too much. Millions would like to lead a quiet, restful, peaceful life. They yearn to relax into easy sleep.

The rapid flight to the suburbs is partly in answer to this. The excitement, opportunity, and diversity of the cities entices, charms, lures our young people; they come in search of jobs and in search of excitement. But the cities themselves have been losing population. We have focused much of our attention on the racial problems involved, but a neglected and fundamental reason has been tensions generated by the cities.

You Can't Run Away and Hide

As we have become more affluent, we have found that neither flights to the suburbs nor soundproofing rooms nor even travel to far-off resort areas that feature a restful, quiet atmosphere can cure the disease of tension and frustration.

Perhaps the problem comes from the competitiveness of our society. Competition in school to get better marks, competition even on the playing fields in everything from Little League baseball to tag and cops-and-robbers. Competition between brothers and sisters, husband and wife, parents and children. Competition is the prime driving force in our enormously productive economic system.

This competition probably has been the most important, progressive, developing influence for what has made this an advanced civilization. But we are becoming aware of the price we have paid for this competition. Some in the oncoming generation are "dropping out" to escape from it.

We Are to Blame

As in so many things, however, the problem is not in what has been most frequently blamed. It's not in our technology, it's not in the driving competition of our economic system, it's not in the speed, noise, rapidity of change in the affluent life we live. *Let's face it, it's in ourselves!* You can be tormented with tension in the midst of the quietest, most restful atmosphere.

Indeed, for the tense personality the absence of the distractions of noise, speed, and competition can become even more terrible.

Consider: When do your tensions really become the most unbearable and difficult? Isn't it when you lie in bed in the quiet and solitude of your room and try to sleep and cannot? Sleeping pills have become a multimillion-dollar business.

The drug industry is increasingly claiming the oncoming generation not only with pep-ups but far more with opiates— for those who seek forgetfulness, relaxation, passiveness, the ability to drift and give in and relax.

When you really think deeply about it, don't you notice that the answer is to teach that organism of yours to let go, to relax, especially when you realize that you can do this not merely in the quiet darkness, the restful, peaceful ease of your bed at night, but in the middle of all the noisy demands on your time and energy, and yes, even at the height of competition?

Relaxation at Will—a Great Talent

Here is why learning to relax in the midst of physical motion, in the middle of the stepped-up roar of the city, learning to do it on signal for as long as you wish, can be such a precious and valuable, indeed a quintessential, capability in this world of ours.

Undoubtedly the ability to relax to the point where heartbeats are slowed and blood pressure is reduced is important. The ability to relax so that sleep can come at will and for as long as you wish is vital. Both are necessary not only to avoid disease and in doing so to prolong life, but especially— and far more importantly—to make the life that is lived bearable. Competition can then become what it should be—a deepening, strengthening element of the relaxed but positive and well-adjusted personality.

You can absorb and enjoy the excitement of entertainment, travel, speed, color, and sound far better with a mind and body and spirit that can relax and let go at regular intervals so you can come on rested, refreshed, strong, and ready.

If this section of the book could teach you nothing but how to sleep (and it can certainly teach you that if you have the patience and will power to stay with it), it would be worthwhile. But it can teach you much more.

Essential to Happiness

Relaxation-at-will is not the be-all and end-all of our health. By itself, relaxation is essentially negative. It's saying No to life, not Yes. It's giving up, not driving ahead. It's letting go and in a sense dying a little instead of holding on and living life more intensely. It's Nay-saying, not Yea-saying.

By itself, relaxation, rest, repose is nothing. The personality that knows how to relax and knows nothing else will vegetate, die, and leave nothing whatsoever behind. All this, however, is said only to put relaxation into perspective. In modern life it is far more essential to know how to relax than ever before, if you are going to become the strong, organized, vital, happy personality that you should be.

It is very difficult indeed these days to teach our bodies to exercise in a prolonged, regular way that gives us the strength, the vitality, the power of heart and circulatory system that will enable us to carry on. It's even more difficult for many of us to learn moderation in eating, to deny ourselves those tasty tidbits whenever we wish them. And perhaps for many it's most difficult of all to learn how to let go, to relax every day and several times every day, and in a special way to learn to relax throughout the day by permitting the muscles and the emotional and mental capabilities that aren't at work to take it easy while the other part of the system is working. Relaxation is at the very crux of achieving health. Without relaxation neither exercise nor diet, except as they contribute to a more rested and relaxed personality, will enable us to win the healthy mind, body, and spirit that happiness requires.

There are two exciting new methods of learning relaxation. Both of them are getting impressive scientific study from outstanding medical experts. One is called biofeedback. The other is transcendental meditation.

28 · Biofeedback—
One Way to Nirvana

ONE OF THE MOST EXCITING new areas of scientific study of the relationship between the will and the mind and body is called biofeedback.

The most prestigious institutions in our country—the Menninger Foundation, Harvard University, the National Institutes of Health—have all begun to get into this area. According to recent research you may be able, if you are very patient and will endure the boredom of daily training for several weeks, to control your heartbeat, your temperature (including the capacity to raise or lower the temperature of one part of your body while keeping another part normal), your blood pressure, and headaches (including even migraine).

Biofeedback has a great future, but in this book I will explore only one phase of it: the new scientific capacity to teach yourself to relax, to sleep, to rest, and to let go whenever you wish, so you are free. You're free to sleep or drift into a restful state of relaxation whenever you wish.

Again—Self-Discipline Is the Price

If you want to be free of the pressure and tension and diversion that keep you awake and tired and tense, here is the way. It's not free. It's not easy. And unless you're a patient and persistent type, or are so highly motivated you're willing to spend the time, forget it.

But it's far better in the long run and in the short run too than the usual relaxants, booze, sleeping pills, tranquilizers. Biofeedback can guarantee no hangover, no addiction, and no reliance on anything except your own strengthened, reinforced, and instructed will.

Does this sound good? Better than dieting or exercise? Well, it may cost you almost as much in time and discipline. And if you want to use one of the new machines it could cost you money.

But with all the new interest—the multimillion-dollar government grants and the comprehensive studies by great educational institutions—there are some old and simple principles of relaxation that are not only not challenged by these new studies of this fascinating aspect of self-control, but are actually reinforced.

You Must Relax

Back in 1908 Dr. Edmund Jacobsen began studying relaxation, and in 1931 he published a simple layman's guide entitled *You Must Relax*. To me this is the classic work in the field. The principle is especially appealing for those of us who have sweated and strained to improve our physical well-being by prolonged physical exertion.

Relaxation is simply the opposite principle. The easiest way to understand how to relax is first to do just what we do when we exercise—that is, tighten up. To understand how to relax, first tense yourself, then let go. Make a tight, tense fist, for instance. Clench your fist just as tightly as you can. Then clench it tighter, until the knuckles whiten with tension and the forearm knots in hard muscular contraction. Feel that tension? Think about it. Prolong it.

Then gradually let go. Let your fist fall open. Let the tension flow out of your fist and your forearm. Observe, savor, reflect on that feeling of letting go.

This is it. This is the heart of relaxing—that letting go. Simple? It is. But it's astounding that many, perhaps most, of our fellow humans don't understand it. Until Jacobsen came along, the word "relax" was barely in our vocabulary.

A Beginning

Letting go is the first principle, but it is far from the last. It is a beginning, a good one, but just that. Jacobsen contributed to relaxation something of the same kind of understanding that Dr. Kenneth Cooper has contributed to exercise. Just as deliberate, prolonged follow-through on exercise is essential for achieving any of the training effects of exercise, so prolonged, patient, persistent follow-through on relaxation is essential for enjoying the benefits of deep, restful, health-restoring relaxation.

Jacobsen shows that letting go and drifting into relaxation requires more than relaxing a tense fist. You pursue that gentle, easy, let-go relaxation mood. You let go further and further. Now this isn't easy for most of us. It's one thing to let your fist fall limp. It's something else to persist in the letting go to deeper levels of relaxation.

And here's where the machine becomes so valuable. You insert paste between electrodes and your skin. You strap the electrodes to your forearm or forehead. You switch on the tension-measuring machine and you let go, you relax. Are you really persisting into deep relaxation? A steady tone of the machine will tell you. As you become tense you lose the tone. As your relaxation returns the tone comes back. You know when you're winning and when you're losing. Your mind comes to recognize, to feed back instantly the thoughts or reveries or attempts to keep your mind empty that lead to success, and what distraction or fantasy frustrates your relaxation.

Rats Are Better at It

You learn, and it's an animalistic learning. In fact some research indicates that rats are better learners in this respect than humans are. Rats can be taught to slow or speed up their heartbeat, to reduce or increase their blood pressure, to increase or lower their temperature. The rat is rewarded with a pleasant jolt in the pleasure portion of its brain when it responds correctly.

Most human beings can be taught these far more complex autonomic controls too, but it takes time and patience. Relaxation is simpler. If you stay with it, you can't lose.

For about five hundred dollars you can buy an efficient machine that will not only measure the extent of your muscle relaxation but provide the basis for steady training. If you don't have the five hundred, don't feel lost. You may be able to use a machine like this at a neighboring university, or possibly your doctor can suggest a hospital or a doctor who has such a machine. If you can arrange to use it long enough to learn muscular relaxation, then you can practice without it.

If you're an eager-beaver organizer, you might even persuade five or six of your neighbors or friends at the office to go in with you to share the cost and the use of the machine.

The Cost

Here's a key to health that costs you more in money than jogging or even swimming. But once again money is only part of the cost. The cost in time, too, is likely to be just as demanding as running or swimming. *Every* day, without exception, you should practice—for weeks.

But there is a difference. Relaxation is a learned skill. Once you've learned it you won't need the machine, although it can be useful to check your continued progress. But for some weeks you will need the will and the planning to use it *daily*.

This needn't carve another half-hour a day out of your life. If you commute to work—after you run—you may be able to set aside a half-hour of that commuting time when you can concentrate on relaxation. You can rise a little earlier, or retire a little earlier, or sleep a little less, or work out a combination. You can probably get along on a little less sleep if you really learn to let go and relax.

Relaxing the Mind

Muscular relaxation is one, but only one, phase. You and I know that the most tortured and frustrating tensions are mental and emotional, not physical. It's that argument with your spouse over the kids, the inconsiderate boss who thoughtlessly insults you by ignoring your good work and cutting you to the quick with your mistakes when you make them. Or maybe it's your tactless remark to a dear friend that you regret and regret and regret. These are emotional hangups.

Then there's the bedeviling problem of your budget—How are you going to meet that insurance premium when you have already committed every dollar of your budget? You go over it again and again. Or something simple and utterly trivial—what was the name of that song you heard in the fifties at your high-school graduation, what are the names of the Los Angeles Rams cornerbacks? These can be the mental teasers that stretch you out, keep you awake.

There's a machine for this too. Surprisingly enough, it's cheaper. For around three hundred and fifty dollars you can buy an efficient and reliable "brain wave" machine that will measure your Alpha waves. Sound nutty? Well, it's not. It's scientifically accepted as a sure way to determine your mental activity.

When your mind is full and concentrating on some mental

or emotional problem, the frequency given off by your brain is in the Beta range, giving off brain waves at 14 to 40 cycles per second. When you slow down, relax, slip into a light, easy reverie, your brain gives off a lower or slower cycle of activity, a relaxed, pleasant state of awareness, and you enter an Alpha stage. Your brain waves vary between 7 and 14. If you slip lower than Alpha you move into Theta, at the borderline of sleep, with your brain-cycle emissions down to 4 to 7 per second. This, of course, is even more relaxed and is harder to achieve. It may be especially creative. Finally, at Delta you are in deep sleep at 0 to 4 cycles per second.

"Alpha" has its advantages as a first step in relaxation training. You are aware, but your mind is floating in an easy neutral; frustrations and annoyances fade away.

The Zen Master View

In Eugèn Herrigel's famous book, *Zen in the Art of Archery,* there is one of the most remarkable of a series of reports on the experience of deep mental relaxation:

> The demand that the door of the senses be closed is not meant by turning energetically away from a sensible world, but rather by a readiness to yield without resistance. In order that this actionless activity may be accomplished instinctively, the soul needs an inner hold and it wins it by *concentrating on breathing.* This is performed consciously with a conscientiousness that borders on the pedantic. *The breathing in, like the breathing out, is practiced again and again by itself with the utmost care.* One does not have to wait long for results. *The more one concentrates on breathing, the more the external stimuli fade into the background.* They sink away in a kind of muffled roar which one hears with only half an ear at first and in the end one finds it no more disturbing than the distinct roar of the sea, which, once one has grown accustomed to it, is no longer perceived. In due course one even grows immune to larger stimuli and at the same time detachment from them comes easier and quicker. Care has only to be taken that the body is relaxed whether standing, sitting or lying, and if one then concentrates on breathing

one soon feels oneself shut in by impermeable layers of silence. *One only knows and feels that one breathes. And to detach oneself from this feeling and knowing, no fresh decision is required for the breath slows down of its own accord, becomes more and more economical in the use of breath, and finally, slipping by degrees into a blurred monotone, escapes one's attention altogether.* [Emphasis Added]

Notice the refreshingly new instruction, new certainly to this sheep counter. You concentrate on breathing. The aficionados of this technique say the way to do this is to count your *ex*halations—that's right, your *ex*halations, not your inhalations—and envision yourself sinking down into your stomach with each exhalation. As you concentrate on counting, your mind is less likely to wander away from breathing.

They suggest a far better way to count than my white, floating sheep lifting gently over a vine-covered fence. For years I relied on that old wives' advice. It wasn't bad, but when I got to something like 1,524 or 1,679 I'd realize how long I'd been at it and that would appall and depress me and I'd give up. The current advice on counting your breath is to go only to ten, then start again at one.

All this should be done in as relaxed and comfortable a position as possible. For that you use the Jacobsen technique to extend the letting go of tension in your fist progressively to your other muscles. First tense, then relax, farther and farther. Go up your arm to your shoulder, then the other arm. Do the same thing with your leg, starting with your toes—right up to your stomach.

My Waterloo has always been my jaw. Maybe because I'm a talkative, sometimes filibustering senator, my jaw muscles get lots of work and they're so tense that I almost unsnap them when I relax. But the limpness of the jaw when I achieve it represents my final victory in relaxation. A happy, easy vision for me in achieving final and total relaxation is to imagine my body as a tired sock draped over the back of a chair, completely limp.

If you can go this far—that is, if you can learn to feel totally relaxed—you'll probably have little trouble sleeping or finding refreshment when you want simply to cave in for a while.

Want to Go Further?

Maybe you'd like to go further with this kind of relaxation. If so, a pleasant new world awaits you—if you have the patience, and if you practice and practice. To quote *Zen in the Art of Archery* again:

> This exquisite state of unconcerned immersion in oneself is not, unfortunately, of long duration. It is liable to be disturbed from the inside. As though sprung from nowhere, moods, feelings, desires, worries and even thoughts incontinently rise up, in a meaningless jumble . . . The only successful way of rendering this disturbance inoperative is to keep on breathing, quietly and unconcernedly, to enter into friendly relations with whatever appears on the scene, to accustom oneself to it, to look at it equably and at last grow weary of looking. In this way one gradually gets into a state which resembles the melting drowsiness of sleep.

Once again, as far as most of us are concerned this is it. Once we can traipse along that road to sleep, what more can we ask? Jacobsen, that grand old man of relaxation, used to define ultimate relaxation as simply sleep. And maybe this is all you want. For most of us it is aplenty.

But maybe not. Perhaps you want to go further on your mental relaxation kick. There's a reward in doing so and the Zen master describes it as follows:

> To slip into it [sleep] finally is a danger which has to be avoided. It [this drowsy stage] is met by a peculiar leap of concentration, comparable perhaps to the jolt which a man who has stayed up all night gives himself when he knows that his life depends on all his senses being alert; and if this leap has been successful but a single time it can be repeated with certainty. With its help the soul is brought to a point where it vibrates of itself in itself—a

serene pulsation which can be heightened into the feeling, otherwise experienced only in rare dreams of extraordinary lightness, and rapturous certainty of being able to summon up energies in any direction, to intensify or release tensions graded to a nicety.

Do You Really Want to Learn?

The big element in whether or not you will learn to relax is, of course, your motivation. You have to understand what good it will do you to go through the long, often boring discipline, the concentrated patience of learning how to turn on or turn off to relaxation. I've already suggested other justifications for going through this training, but consider something that motivates almost all of us—your appearance—and more than your appearance, your personality.

Consider what relaxing does for you. The tense lines in your face become gentle and soft. Your squinted eye and furrowed forehead smooth into a composed serenity. It is no wonder that almost all the great portraits from the *Mona Lisa* on are composed and relaxed. When the expert photographer "shoots" you, one reason why he snaps so many pictures is to catch you in a relaxed, serene, composed attitude. Probably the main advantage of the candid shot is that you lose the tenseness of self-consciousness. You forget that you're "on." Your nervous How-do-I-look? tautness gives way to the distraction of a joke.

And, you know how a tense jaw, a trembling hand, an erratic but constant movement gives your lack of composure away. You've seen it in yourself and in those you have talked with.

As for personality, the tense, taut, tight person comes on artificially. He just doesn't seem natural. And, of course, he isn't. He's forced.

The Relaxed Speaker

As a senator I'm especially conscious of the matter of relaxation when I speak or hear a colleague speak. The relaxed speaker may have nothing to say but he can still be a delight. The warmth of his personality comes through. As a speaker you know when you have won an audience because you can relax with it. This may be wholly irrelevant to the merits of what you say, but if your audience feels your tension, they may pity you, but they are far less likely to listen to you or be convinced.

At a time when an increasing number of people feel there's something artificial or at least superficial and "irrelevant" about looking your best and being concerned about appearance—and maybe you're one of them—here's another motivation that may turn you on.

Consider: *You cannot be angry and relaxed at the same time.* Think about that. Try it. You can't do it. The advice to the angry man or woman to "relax" makes good sense. That's exactly what you should do when you want to let the anger flow out.

Now reflect on this with me. Why isn't the same principle true of any emotion that comes from hatred or jealousy or bitterness or just plain irritability? These are the emotions that make us tense, the emotions that keep us tense, and in turn, the juice of our bitterness, jealousy, hatred, irritability reinforce our tension, keep it alive. Buy it?

If not, consider the positive. How much easier it is to be gentle, loving, tender when you're relaxed.

Certainly there's infinitely more to human relations than the simple physical act of being composed and relaxed. Love is far stronger and deeper than any program for easing the muscles and brain can explain. But surely a prime prerequisite for getting along happily, warmly, for being helpful and loving, is to develop the capacity to relax and let the irritation, the anger, the bitterness go, to know how to let it go.

You take a simple, physical first step toward letting it go when you develop the capacity to relax whenever you wish to. And you prepare for at least the potentiality of friendlier and happier relationships with others.

Relax and Reduce

Consider another good reason for relaxing. This one ties in with your diet.

Many of us eat for the same reason we smoke.

I say that as a nonsmoker. I'm told by many people that when they are tense, nervous, working hard, under pressure, they smoke much more. We nonsmokers (and smokers too) often eat for the same reason.

This is an understandable distraction and undoubtedly hundreds of thousands, perhaps millions, of people are plagued by a nervous habit that gives them unwanted weight and destroys the joy of eating for the pleasure of satisfying hunger.

Here's another reason to learn how to relax, to turn off your tensions as you would snap your fingers. When you are tempted to reach for a potato chip, a soft drink, a cookie, a piece of candy, try this instead: Get up, walk around, let those tensions ease out.

It's not easy when you're active, but that's another aspect of effective relaxation.

Relax in Action

It's one thing to be able to relax when you're sitting in a quiet room or lying quietly in bed; it's something else to relax when you are mobile. But it can be done. By far the best athletic competitors are those who compete all out and at the same time are relaxed.

It can't be done? It is done. It is done even in such tense and dangerous sports as boxing.

For five years in high school and four years in college I

boxed every winter. I found that as my confidence grew and as I became a better boxer, I was able to relax, to go through a fight without even breathing hard, while throwing more punches and moving faster than my opponent. The answer was not condition, because sometimes I was not in better condition than the man I was boxing. The answer was that I was relaxed—without at that time knowing it.

As I indicate elsewhere in this book, you can not only learn to run, walk, swim, while relaxed; you can do these things much better if you are relaxed.

And as for the intellectual tasks, public speaking, debating, the clash of personality against personality, you will perform far better if you are physically at ease, composed and relaxed.

If you find that as you work at a demanding, frustrating, irritating job in your home or in your office you are using food as a crutch, the answer is the same answer you should seek when you are angry. RELAX. Just let go. Become conscious of your muscles in your jaw, in your arm, your hands, your legs, and let them sag. You can learn it and help kill that appetite.

29 · Transcendental Meditation for a Serene Future

A FRONT-PAGE ARTICLE in the *Wall Street Journal* in August of 1972 hailed transcendental meditation as a technique for relaxation that is truly mushrooming in popularity.

The article reported:

> Thousands of otherwise conservative businessmen, scientists, teachers and housewives have taken up the practice, reporting such beneficial effects as freedom from tension, mental well-being and heightened energy and creativity. Although skeptics abound, they seem to be far outnumbered by converts and true believers. And, lending a new respectability to the practice, are doctors and researchers at universities and hospitals.

One estimate at that time placed the number of meditators at 150,000, with the number growing at the rate of 5,000 per month. The technique is now being promoted by a group called the International Meditation Society.

In the *Wall Street Journal* article, Ellen Graham describes the technique as follows:

> Instruction in Transcendental Meditation is available at IMS centers in most cities. During training each participant meets privately with a teacher and is assigned a mantra, or meaningless sound, which the IMS will define only by calling it "the vehicle that allows meditation to take place." (There are different mantras for different people, although the group won't say how many mantras there are or on what basis they are assigned.)

Sitting upright in a chair with eyes closed, the student listens to his mantra as it is chanted by his teacher, and then silently. During meditation, the muscles in the body relax, and may even twitch involuntarily. The head sometimes slumps forward. Meditators appear for all practical purposes to be asleep. Yet they say their minds remain acutely aware of outside stimuli, such as movements or noise in the room. The process is completely natural and involves no effort, meditators claim.

What goes on during meditation differs with each person, but one practiced meditator describes her experience like this: "You close your eyes, and after a few minutes the mantra just floats into your consciousness. Sometimes noises or mundane daydreams may distract you, but then you find your mind wandering back to the mantra. You feel a deep sense of rest and alertness pass through your mind and body." Practitioners say the meditative response begins as soon as the mind turns to the mantra. But how the mantra actually works—if indeed, anyone knows —is a well kept secret.

Obviously the physical effects of transcendental meditation are similar, though not identical, to (1) relaxation by the old Jacobsen method of tensing and then progressively and at length easing tension in muscle after muscle; and (2) the biofeedback technique of conditioning by using machines to persuade the body and mind to respond to sounds and lights until conditioned relaxation becomes second nature. The description in the preceding chapter of the Zen master's relaxation by counting exhalations with an easy let-go, passive concentration is also similar.

Completely Natural

The prime advantage of so-called transcendental meditation is that key sentence: "The process is completely natural and involves no effort."

In a sense this is true of all means of achieving relaxation. In fact, "letting go" is the opposite of effort.

So the purpose of all systems of relaxation is to let the tensions drift away and subside. Whatever will induce you to have the patience—to take the time to establish the confidence that ultimately you will find relaxation—whatever method you adopt is less significant than your staying with it.

In this transcendental meditation seems to be having unusual success today, partly, I suppose, because it has become commercial. When you have invested seventy-five dollars in four two-hour lessons, when you have worked with a teacher and talked over your failures and successes with others, you have established the basis for a very considerable motivation that is likely to give you the patience, the confidence, the persistence to stay with it until you have won the self-control that enables you to relax on your own signal, as you will it.

Transcendental meditation has begun to prove itself impressively. One Wall Street broker reported that after meditating for more than a year he found himself a far happier person, in harmony with his surroundings, without anxiety, and less critical of other people.

Incidentally, the broker found his meditation time on the commuter train going home each evening.

Measurable Benefits

Dr. Herbert Benson, of the faculty of Harvard University Medical School, tested a group of meditators and found that during meditation the meditators' blood pressure was low, heart and respiration slowed—measurable physiological effects that are the very opposite of stress. In stress your blood pressure speeds up, your heart beats faster as your anxiety increases. Another indication of the provable physical effect of meditation was the measurable increase in Alpha brain waves, evidence of a relaxed, rested state.

The Benson finding shows that transcendental meditation is a provably useful method of achieving relaxation, not simply a matter of suggestion. And TM, as it is being called, seems sure to be on its way to much bigger and better things as a system of natural, drug-free adjustment to our tense, exacting world.

The technique has already been tried in the Eastchester, New York, public schools. The school began offering TM instruction on a voluntary basis for high-school students. A few teachers and 15 to 20 percent of the students took the course. Guidance counselors reported impressive results: Meditators got better grades, stopped using drugs, were more outgoing, and got along better with their parents, teachers, and friends.

Courses in "The Science of Creative Intelligence," the theoretical framework behind the practice of TM, are already being offered for credit in some of the nation's great universities, including Yale, Stanford, and Colorado.

Biofeedback may not catch on as the best method of learning relaxation, and transcendental meditation as currently structured may be replaced by some more efficient and attractive approach. On the other hand, each of these systems may thrive and grow. And they could grow explosively.

Relaxation Has a Great Future

But whether or not these particular techniques are the answer to learning to relax at will so that you can rest and sleep and refresh your body, mind, and spirit when you wish—without drugs—some such method is coming and it's coming with a rush. We need it. Mental disorders, alcoholism, the pathetic tragedy of drug addiction all call out for this.

Relaxation as a part of our way of life is coming—and no one is going to hold it back. The question is whether we will learn to coordinate the use of that relaxation with the use of tension, to blend and alternate tension and letting-stress-go, so that our creativity and achievement can progress.

30 · Relax *While* You Work!

W<small>HEN</small> <small>SENATOR</small> <small>JOHN</small> <small>PASTORE</small> delivers a rousing speech on the floor of the Senate—and no one, but no one, can match him—he obviously isn't limp and languid. But he's just as obviously not under the stress of anxiety or tension. John can have the usually bored Senate and press gallery rollicking with laughter, attentive and fascinated. He can play to this most difficult of all audiences like a musician. He has a gift.

But how about the inner Pastore? How does this best-of-all Senate orators do it?

First, let's face it, Pastore speaks under a kind of emotional pressure. He obviously feels what he has to say and he lets his emotions move him, guide him, and flow out of him. He uses emotion to persuade, entertain, shame, or inspire us. His face gets red, the words come in a rush, he clenches his fist, and flails his arms. It's a beautiful performance that you have to hear and see to believe. This is one of the rare times when senators stream out of the cloakroom onto the floor to hear a Senate speech instead of reversing that route. But all of the Pastore emotion is centered on the message. There is no self-conscious anxiety causing tension. He has little or no concern that listeners may be critical of him or how he speaks. His concentration is evident. It is not complicated and intensified by self-doubt or anxiety.

In this chapter I want to discuss an exciting new step in

relaxation that you may find far more useful when you are working under stress, even physical stress.

It may seem unnatural and contradictory, if not impossible, to relax while you're walking, running, doing physical work, or making a speech, but you can. And your performance will greatly improve if you learn how to do it.

Try It While Walking

After you have developed the capacity to ease muscular tension at will and under quiet circumstances, and after you have learned to release the emotional and mental frustrations that plague you by slipping into an Alpha state of mental meditation and reverie, try applying the same principles in your walking.

This doesn't mean that you have to amble. You can relax while you are walking vigorously if you let every muscle that isn't at work lose its tension and let go. It may be easier to begin this kind of relaxation when you're doing such simple physical work as walking. I sometimes find it even easier to let a frustrating emotional problem drift away during a walk than when I lie in bed at night.

While you walk, switch your mental gears into neutral by doing something simple like counting your exhalations or observing the people and things you pass while you're walking. If disturbing thoughts cross your mind, don't resist them, just move away from them in your mind. You will find that after a little while your mind is composed. You may find, as many do, that your fist is clenched when you walk. Let it go, just let it flop easily and relax as you would in a quiet room. Let your jaw and forehead go limp.

Walking requires your big muscles. It requires more from some of them than from others. Your arms swinging at your sides help you walk. They can swing loosely and easily, as relaxed as possible. Reflect on how you push yourself ahead with each stride. Only the muscle of the leg that is pushing needs to contract in tension. Your other leg can let go, and should. Relaxing as you swing the other leg in place is easy, and you'll find it much easier if your mind is relaxed.

What you do in walking you can do in the same way in running.

Running too requires only some of your muscles at work. Sprinting requires close to full stress, but running at any easy pace or jogging can be relaxing. Your arms, shoulders, chest help you run but they can help in an easy, rhythmic, relaxed way. Of course your lungs must work hard to pump oxygen into your hard-working legs, but if you don't run too hard and fast, and if you establish an easy rhythm, you will find that even your lungs will relax.

Again, the principal tool you have for this relaxation is your brain. You can gentle it into neutral, let it out to attain that Alpha floating feeling, and it will communicate itself to your muscles so they will work as much as they need to but no more.

Relaxed Swimming

Unless you have done a lot of swimming, you may think it impossible to relax when you are swimming hard and reasonably fast. But I find that nothing contributes more to the delight of swimming than shifting the mind into an Alpha state and letting the arms and legs alternately pull with effort and ease into relaxation. It takes time and practice, but once again the key is in mental attitude. Your chest, your arms, your legs, your stomach muscles are alternately at work and at ease if your mind is at ease.

The remarkable effect of this kind of relaxation is that your fatigue is greatly reduced. Your muscles work but they also rest. You enjoy mental relaxation and it simply cannot come to those who fail to exercise, at least not in the same degree. Your whole system—your heart, your lungs, even your psyche—concentrates on the exercise and there is little left over for the tensions and stresses of psychological or mental problems. Learn to relax this way and you're well on your way to real enjoyment of exercise.

This principle applies not only to the prolonged kind of exercise I advocate in this book. It certainly applies to golf, tennis, baseball, football, and virtually all the other sports we engage in.

The good golfer competing in a tournament is under enormous pressure. He couldn't possibly control his body if he didn't know how to relax. He may never even have thought of relaxation, but he does it. And if you don't believe it, watch him. Just imagine what would have happened to Arnold Palmer or Jack Nicklaus or Lee Trevino if they were as tense as you and I would be in playing seventy-two holes of golf when thousands of dollars ride on every putt, drive, and chip shot. Talk about a prescription for a nervous breakdown! The answer is that these men know how to relax, as all good athletes do.

Relax at Work

Far more important than learning how to relax in sports is learning how to relax in your work. Physical work requires exactly the same principle I have discussed with respect to walking, running, swimming. It's a matter of simply letting the muscles that aren't at work take it easy. This is true if you're making a bed, sweeping a floor, hammering a nail, mowing a lawn, or even lifting a weight. If the activity is very brief, of course, the need for relaxation is far less important.

If your work is like mine, a matter of talking and working with people, listening to witnesses, studying, and speaking, you will find relaxation infinitely helpful in your performance. There are superb speakers who can read, assimilate, understand the most complicated matters. Some people can listen calmly to boring or irrelevant witnesses without knowing or caring a thing about relaxation. If they thought about it, if they carefully analyzed their mental and physical state, they would find they were reasonably relaxed. But even with those who are naturally good, performance can be improved by deliberate, planned relaxation.

Senate Hearing

Take a senator sitting in a hearing as I do day after day, listening to a witness who may have enormously important information but is presenting it in a dull way. Your first step is to be physically relaxed and alert. This means concentrating on the substance of what the witness is saying by knowing as much about it as you can before the testimony begins, and this is why in the Senate we require our witnesses to have their statements on file before the committee twenty-four hours before they appear. Those of us who are conducting the hearing have a chance to study the testimony so that we understand it, know what to look for, and are in a position to question the witness. This preparation and concentration helps you to be composed, without a shaking or trembling hand, without your fist gripping the side of the chair, without any of the physical tautness or tension that tires and drains you.

It's not listening to the witness that exhausts a senator, it's the nervous habit of physical tension. With practice, relaxation can come just as easily when you're sitting in a hearing room listening to an important witness with the kleig lights of television on, as when you're lying quietly in your bed or sitting in a quiet room. It takes a little reflection, easing of your muscular tensions, and concentration on the substance of what the witness is saying.

Reading

It may seem unnecessary to suggest that you can relax while reading, but reading can be stimulative, provocative, exciting, and even nerve-racking. Yes, physical habits can exhaust you even when you're reading. If you are comfortable, with easy physical relaxation, your muscles as easy as if you're going to sleep, you can focus on reading and comprehend it more readily and swiftly than if you're tense.

Reading can provide a relaxing change of pace from physical activity. Why? Because your muscles that were laboring can let go. Your mind that was at ease can pick up. After a long run, I find that reading—even if the material is complicated or technical—is refreshing.

Public Speaking

Many people who aren't in public life feel that the most nerve-racking and frightening aspect of it must be public speaking. Actually it's one of the easiest parts of being a United States Senator and one of the most pleasant. As a matter of fact, many of us in the business enjoy speaking so much that we become bores and speak too much!

But there's no reason why speaking before any kind of audience under any circumstances should ever be nerve-racking for anyone.

Winston Churchill wrote that he used to have trouble speaking before an audience until he overcame his nervousness by simply recognizing that he knew much more about the subject than most or all of the people listening to him. When he realized how ignorant they were, self-confidence would come and nervousness would leave.

This kind of personal psyching up may be necessary for you. If you know your subject, you can be physically relaxed the same way you are, as I have just suggested, when you walk, run, swim, listen, or read. You will find that speaking while relaxed is simply a matter of developing confidence by practicing. Even with senators the performance varies a great deal. I am a far better speaker at the end of a campaign than at the beginning. It's a matter of getting into the easy swing of things so that the thoughts come readily.

It may seem impossible or even ridiculous to think you can relax your mental processes as well as your physical processes while speaking, and of course you can't slip into Alpha or Delta states unless you talk in your sleep—which isn't exactly the best prescription for public speaking. What you can do is to lose anxieties, feelings of inadequacy, fears of possible failure. You can do this by knowing your subject well and recognizing that you know it probably as well as or better than your audience does, by recalling your speaking successes, by slowing down your rate of speech (nervous, tense speakers often talk very rapidly), by doing your best to enjoy what you say yourself (enjoying any jokes you may have, enjoying the clarity with which you make a point), by pausing, feeling the audience respond.

Meanwhile, forget about yourself and any critical reaction your audience may have, except to remember that virtually any audience wants to like you as a speaker. The worst thing that can happen is that they may forget that you spoke or what you said, and after all, what's so bad about that?

In an earlier section we talked about posture. I should mention again that it's possible to relax by walking tall or sitting tall, head erect, shoulders back, stomach drawn in, pelvis tilted forward. That may still sound contradictory, but it's the acme of effective relaxation.

Muhammed Ali vs. Joe Frazier

You can see the capacity to relax under tension and pressure beautifully in a boxing match between two real professionals. When men like Muhammed Ali and Joe Frazier fight, they can go fifteen rounds at close to top speed, dealing out punishment so enormous that marathon runners, who are in far better condition, would be exhausted by the end of four or five rounds.

How can they do it? The answer, of course, is that hundreds of rounds of sparring and boxing have taught them how to relax in this trying, almost traumatic experience of facing someone who can not only annihilate you with one punch but is trying his best to do it.

It's very likely that neither Joe Frazier nor Muhammed Ali has ever thought of the Alpha waves of the brain or even of the Jacobsen system of aggressive relaxation. But in their specialty, they both obviously know how to practice it.

There is no reason why this technique of being able to turn on relaxation, or rather, turn off tension, shouldn't become a great boon to all of us in the future.

Basketball

However impressed I am with the ability of a professional boxer to relax, I'm sure that many Americans are more impressed by the fantastic ability of professional basketball players to go at top speed.

Those who have played pro basketball have found it to be one of the most exhausting games there is. How do they get that speed? Endurance tests of the top basketball stars when they're in training indicate that their distance running is mediocre or worse, and yet they can keep running on a basketball floor in a way that would exhaust Jim Ryun or Kip Keino. Why? Because they relax with a confidence born of experience.

There are few sports that require a greater degree of constant alertness than basketball, with its rapid-fire motion, passing, shooting, intercepting passes, blocking. It's an exciting, fast-moving game to watch, and it is also one that requires tremendous endurance and physical condition.

Millions of Americans have played basketball and know

how tiring even a few minutes can be if you go all out. And you can imagine what this does in professional basketball when you're up against the best in the business.

Watch the top basketball players when they are not actually moving down the floor and you'll see a picture of concentrated, alert relaxation, every muscle at ease. The motion, when it comes, is smooth, effortless, and only as fast as it has to be. This is something that comes to basketball players after years and years of play, and after developing through years of high school and college and then professional play.

I doubt if relaxation, as such, is ever taught. In basketball, as in boxing and running, it doesn't have to be. Your muscles automatically acquire it. But if you're not a practiced athlete you can very quickly achieve this same advantage of resting and easing your muscles, putting them under both stress and relaxation while swimming, walking, and running, if you go at it consciously as I've indicated in this chapter.

Stress

Regardless of what I have just written about Muhammed Ali, Joe Frazier, and pro basketball stars, let's not kid ourselves. When any one of them is operating at his best—when Joe throws that ferocious left hook to the chin and follows with a right to the solar plexus and another left to the chin (that dazzling combination!)—he is operating under real stress. When Dave Wottle or Frank Liquori comes down the stretch in the last hundred yards of the mile or fifteen-hundred meters, he's under enormous stress. Indeed, all the great accomplishments of our time, almost every deed which is enshrined in history, was achieved through immense stress.

And stress has its benefits. You can't develop a strong, hard bicep muscle without the stress of lifting weights, of isometric exercises that intensify stress. You can't develop a quick, incisive mental capacity without the stress involved in stressful mental effort on complicated mental problems.

In the razzmatazz world of television such people as Dick Cavett, Jack Paar, and Johnny Carson respond with their warm, congenial personalities and their quick minds in immensely stressful situations. Millions of television listeners, including more than a few thousand who are haters, hang on every word. The excellence of their performance is a matter of years of practice under the pressure cooker, being required to make ad-lib responses to totally unexpected situations and extraordinarily difficult questions.

Stress starts the adrenalin flowing and this energizes the brain and body. It provides the tense atmosphere necessary to achievement.

Costs of Relaxation

There are costs of relaxation. It may well be that many Americans are just too relaxed too much of the time; relaxed in the sense that they are flopped limp in the chair before the television set, their minds passively absorbing whatever comes through on the boob-tube. After all, relaxation is strictly negative. It is not a matter of catching on. It is a matter of letting go. It is not a matter of pushing ahead, but of easing up, caving in, drifting effortlessly in a dreamy reverie.

If stress is the prime prerequisite for achievement, relaxation by itself achieves nothing. You are almost completely relaxed when you are asleep. One way you can be totally and surely relaxed is to be absolutely, coldly dead. Say what you want to about rigor mortis, when you are dead, all tensions are gone. Relaxation is total.

Now I've just given you the best that can be said for stress and the worst that can be said for relaxation. Let's briefly reverse it.

Stress, and stress by itself without relaxation, undoubt-edly leads to breakdowns, trembling, inept performance, fatigue, heart disease, and untimely death.

On the other hand, relaxation should have all the benefits I've discussed earlier, including not only the delight of ease and sleep and the pleasure of drifting reverie, but a healthier body, a body that's less likely to suffer heart attacks and other diseases as well as headaches, strokes, and so forth.

Answer: Combine Stress and Relaxation

We need to learn to use stress and relaxation in tandem, use them together in almost everything we do. The principle should be to achieve your goal, which always requires a certain degree of stress, and at the same time to pace yourself so that you don't wear yourself out.

This may not be easy. There's a constant temptation, whether you're running, speaking, listening, or studying, to improve your performance by stepping up the tension. But running faster, speaking faster, can become counterproduc-tive, exhausting. With the best conditioning we can't sustain maximum stress for more than a very short time.

The combination of stress and relaxation requires pacing. It requires, above all, recognizing the *irrelevancy* of every tension that is not directly related to the achievement of your particular goal. Just as Joe Frazier's arms and legs are relaxed when he's not throwing punches, all his energy, all his drive goes into that magnificent left hand to the jaw.

Similarly, John Pastore has no anxiety as to what other senators will think about him or whether he's going to be interrupted or contradicted in a way that he can't answer. Pastore's anxieties are nil when he delivers a speech. All he thinks about is the message, and that's why he's so good.

I never heard Bob La Follette, the great Senator from Wisconsin who served a brilliant twenty years in the Senate early in this century. But Old Bob was able to speak for four or five hours loudly and strenuously without any sign of fatigue. I'm sure it was because the tensions that bother the inexperienced speaker, the fear, the concern, the anxiety, were completely gone when Bob took the stump.

Change-of-Pace Method

Another way of looking at the relaxation-in-motion principle is to consider rest through change, that is, not by ceasing activity but by changing activity.

I've already mentioned how a long, hard exercise followed by a session of concentrated study can make both the exercise and the study more restful. Similarly, a relaxed athlete will rest, ease, let go the tension in a muscle that isn't actually at work.

This is most obvious in the distance runner. His right leg is tense when it's working and pushing ahead, but the next fraction of a second it's fully relaxed as the left leg takes over.

In my first campaign for governor of Wisconsin back in 1952, I remember making twenty-five speeches a day. That's right, twenty-five! I made them on different street corners in Milwaukee and in the surrounding cities. Street-corner speaking is a thing of the past now, for that kind of campaign, but up to the 1960s it was taken for granted.

Strangely enough, I was less tired at the end of the day than at the beginning. The answer, of course, is that I was completely relaxed. I knew just what I wanted to say, and I wasn't worried about crowd reaction. Between speeches I was able to give in fully to rest as we drove from one corner to another and I sat quietly in the car.

There was stress—plenty of it—but there was lots of relaxation, too.

For a couple of thousand years Western civilization has been dominated by that remarkable conception of Aristotle, that virtue is a matter of finding a mean between the extremes, not pushing a good thing too far. For example, Aristotle argued that you can have too much courage and push it too far, that too much courage becomes foolhardiness. You can even push honesty too far by insisting on speaking out tactlessly and cruelly, but honestly, about the shortcomings of others.

Stress is the name of the game in life. It's what it's all about. It's what we live for. This is the way we have built a great country and a great civilization. But many of us have carried it too far. The answer, of course, is to temper stress with relaxation.

It doesn't mean not to try harder, but to try harder while relaxing whatever part of your being is not being used to achieve your goal.

31 · Relax into Sleep

PICTURE THIRTY SENATORS stretched out on cots in various stages of undress, a few in pajamas, a few in underwear, some wearing trousers, shirt, and socks but with shoes, jackets, and ties discarded—two or three snoring quietly and one ringing the welkin with loud snorts.

The setting was the Old Supreme Court Chamber, about a hundred feet from the Senate floor, now used as a hearing room.

The senators were snatching a fitful night's sleep because the Southerners had decided to filibuster a civil-rights bill and Lyndon Johnson, then the Majority Leader of the Senate, in turn decided to hold the Senate in continuous twenty-four-hour sessions for six consecutive days to hammer the bill through. Johnson's forces won and the country received its second major civil-rights bill in eighty years.

But to win, a majority of senators had to stay within a few minutes of the floor, so that when the Southerners noted the absence of a majority of senators from the floor, senators could be aroused and brought to the floor to answer to their names and prevent adjournment.

A senator would sleep for an hour or two, awaken to the raucus ringing of two persistent buzzers, put on his clothes and stumble a hundred feet to the floor, respond to his name, then stumble a hundred feet back to his cot to snatch another couple of hours before the next quorum call.

Some senators slept in their offices. A few simply went home and forgot the whole thing. The southern senators could be absent unless they were among those required to be on the floor to speak or to relieve the Speaker if he tired. The result was that the southerners lost only part of one night's sleep while the rest of the senators suffered through six nights of irregular and broken sleep.

Penalties of Sleeplessness

The effect on disposition, efficiency, and cooperation was evident. A few senators spoke of health being undermined. This was usually expressed as concern about the health of other senators, some of the "older men."

As one of the senators who lived through that minor ordeal, I think it underlined the grossly exaggerated attitude that some of the most intelligent, thoughtful, and informed members of our society have toward sleep.

Don't get me wrong, sleep is a delight and undoubtedly a significant element in health. But somehow almost all of us tend to exaggerate its importance.

Sleep isn't like food and exercise. Your body will tell you when it's tired and wants to go to sleep and it will sleep just about as long as it needs to. Few people in ordinary circumstances have died or even become ill because of lack of sleep. It's easy to overeat and underexercise, but it's rare that you get too little sleep, or for that matter, get too much.

Nevertheless, all of us are troubled at one time or another, and some more than others, by the need for sleep and the desire for the ultimate relaxation that only sleep gives. For most of us it doesn't come automatically or last as long as we would like, and we all know we feel tired and irritable when we consistently go with too little sleep. Our resistance drops, we get colds and even more serious illnesses.

How to Sleep

The fundamental answer is the simple Jacobsen let-go principle. You can't go to sleep by positively and directly willing it. You have to go to sleep by giving in, letting go, and reversing the tension; by clenching the fist and then gradually letting it get more and more relaxed and doing the same with the foot, the ankle, the calf, the thigh, both legs, the stomach, the chest, and then when you feel comfortable and relaxed following the technique I've described, counting your exhalations to ten and then counting again.

There are many other contributions to sleep, however, and one of the best was suggested to me when I was a student at the Harvard Graduate School of Business Administration. One of my friends was Walter Cummings, who has since become a distinguished judge in Chicago. Walter, an excellent student, followed a different sleep principle from the rest of us. He would stop all his studying or other rigorous mental activity at 9:00 P.M., refusing to do anything disturbing after that hour. That's not a bad prescription.

The Healing Power of Sleep

Recent Russian experiments with hospital patients have found that the most effective therapy is to encourage patients to relax and sleep as much as possible. To the best of my knowledge, this is one of the few scientifically controlled sleep studies, and I understand that it indicates that sleep is a specific therapy which can heal, retard disease, and improve health.

In view of the universal interest in sleep, and the popular opinion of the importance of sleep, it is astonishing that so little work has been done in this area. Most studies of sleep have concentrated on the different levels of sleep, the timing and use of dreams. But few have sought to find out the effect on health of a modest increase of sleep.

Exercise

How can we get the kind of restful sleep we want without sleeping tablets, booze, or other crutches? Consider exercise. I have found that of steady, regular, prolonged exercise, walking is the best, though running and swimming are excellent too. Exercise that genuinely fatigues the muscles represents a remarkable natural sleep inducer.

An unusual fallout benefit from exercise has surprised me. I have found that I need less sleep when I'm engaged in prolonged exercise than when I'm not. Perhaps that's because the sleep is deeper when you're physically tired.

Diet, too, plays a role in sleep. In my own experience a heavy meal is likely to disturb sleep. The combination of vigorous exercise and light eating somehow makes the muscles and the nervous system demand sleep and lets sleep come more easily.

But relaxation on signal, the self-discipline of being able to let go physically and mentally, is undoubtedly the biggest and best contributor to falling asleep and to going back to sleep when you awaken in the middle of the night. I've found that as I grow older it's easier for me to fall asleep. I also waken after three or four hours and sometimes have a little difficulty going back to sleep. There are several ways to deal with this. One is to relax systematically and patiently and let go. Another is to take advantage of the blissful solitude and quiet of those late-night hours and concentrate on doing some work.

After four or five hours of restful sleep, I may wake up and begin to think over a debate or discussion on the floor of the Senate or in committee the day before. I switch on the light, reach over for my tape recorder, and sometimes for the next hour or two dictate a memorandum which is often the best work I've done during the entire week. It may be a speech, it may be simply a background paper to remind me how to meet the problem in the future. Usually that means that I will get little sleep the rest of the night and have to settle for four and a half or five hours of sleep. But I have found that, just as I am able to function efficiently after abstaining from food for a day, I can run my five miles and swim without any particular feeling of fatigue. Without exception, the night after a short sleep I sleep soundly the night through.

I think a great deal of our concern and worry over inability to go back to sleep is based on the faulty assumption that the body will suffer and health will break because you didn't get enough sleep. This is unlikely to be so because your body, if it is normal and reasonably healthy, will simply demand the sleep it needs.

Need for Sleep Varies

How much sleep you need varies so much that the rules just can't be established. The most conspicuous example of this I've ever known is Senator Hubert H. Humphrey. Hubert is able to go at full tilt, arguing brilliantly on the floor, negotiating in committee, always in high good humor after working very hard in the Senate or on the campaign trail. He's the last one to miss a happy social occasion. Yet Hubert never seems to be tired. He's a bundle of astonishing energy.

Unfortunately, I can't say that Senator Humphrey is the product of the Proxmire principles in this book. He's not particularly interested in exercise. He's been a little overweight, although lately he's brought his weight down. Diet is certainly not the answer. And he has never developed any interest in systematic, disciplined relaxation.

So if you're Hubert Humphrey, you can just forget the messages here. But if you're a normal kind of person who gets tired, fat, and slows down, and if you haven't found that mysterious Humphrey Fountain of Youth, this book should help.

The Presidents' Way

In recent years White House physicians have advised United States Presidents to husband their energy in a remarkable way. This has interested me very much because, of course, the President does have the most exacting, demanding, frustrating as well as most important job in the world.

To maintain our Presidents' health and keep their energy and alertness at high levels, White House doctors have almost always advised them to take a very long nap in the middle of the day.

This was true of President Truman, President Kennedy, and President Johnson. Whether it's true of Presidents Eisenhower and Nixon I don't know, as I have been less privy to the health secrets of the Republican Presidents.

When I say a long nap in the middle of the day, I mean it. The White House doctors would have our Presidents pull down the shades, take off their clothes, get into their pajamas, and get in bed just as if they were going to sleep for the night. They would sleep for as much as three or four hours every day.

I recall Spessard Holland, the former Senator from Florida, complaining that when President Johnson gave a soiree he was able to dance far into the night because he'd had three or four hours of refreshing sleep before the party began.

Most of us lack the sovereign control of the President. Senators have far more ability to order their working lives than most, but we are unable to take three or four hours off in the afternoon for slumber. Most of us, though, can sneak fifteen or twenty minutes, sometimes even an hour, for a nap on the office couch.

Try a Nap a Day

I do this whenever I can. It is a habit my father also followed, a refresher that enabled him to work fourteen hours a day, seven days a week, for the more than fifty years he practiced medicine. I find that it also helps me to work long hours under pressure.

If you can arrange it, try it. It is not easy for most people to nap during the work day, and if you can't do that, I suggest that the next-best way to break up the day is this: Just as soon as you come home at night, before you have dinner, before you watch television, take a few minutes— ten, fifteen, maybe a half-hour—for a nap. You'll find that it makes the evening more restful and pleasant.

I know I'm prescribing a whale of a lot when I suggest that you take time to relax systematically, take time for prolonged exercise, and now take time for a nap. But if you can shift some time from your television or cocktail or beer bull sessions, I think you'll find it well worth while.

Sleep and Longevity

With all our concern about sleep, and considering the fact that we spend nearly a third of our lives at it, it is astonishing that little has been written about its relationship to longevity.

Can you add active years to your life by simply reducing the sleep you get? Maybe you can. But others say this can lead to a shortening of the number of years you live. If any study has been made of this, I don't know, and I think the best answer is simply to experiment gently and gradually to see how short a sleep you can comfortably manage. If you're getting eight hours, you may be able to get along with seven.

Perhaps I should reemphasize that Russian experiment which showed an apparent scientific relationship between sleep and recovery from disease. As for the relationship between vitality and sleep, almost all of us are sure of it. We know that if you get sufficient sleep you do feel more alert and energetic. But where is the proof? All of us know by ample personal experience that inadequate sleep leads to fatigue and irritability and often a carping, unpleasant disposition. We can see the change clearly in little children but we can sense it in ourselves. And when we've failed to get adequate sleep, many of us show it immediately in our appearance. We get circles under the eyes, a pale, sallow color.

Sleep—good, restful, long sleep, whenever you want it or need it—is certainly one of the best arguments for cultivating the capacity to relax fully, completely, and whenever you wish.

32 · Your Happiness Day

THE PHYSICAL METHODS I have described so far seem to me essential to understanding and achieving relaxation. If you practice these techniques enough, you'll be able to relax at will. Nothing can keep you from eventually becoming composed and at ease. You'll have more energy to concentrate on the task at hand. You'll be much better able to recover physically and mentally from the periods of stress that are inevitable in this high-tempo age and that are essential for real accomplishment.

Take It Easy

But this may not be enough for you. It certainly shouldn't be enough for most of us. We need something more and we can find it in the kind of day-to-day common-sense advice that we get so often on how to relax. What I'm talking about is that fine cliché, "Take it easy." The trouble with that advice is that if we don't know how to take it easy it doesn't mean anything. The preceding discussion of how to relax should take care of a big part of that. Now you know how to relax.

The second difficulty is that we hear this expression so often we pay no attention to it. Like so many clichés, it's a greeting or expression which often doesn't register. Once we know how to relax physically, once we have developed the techniques that we have just described, we can really begin to take it easy.

But taking it easy is not only a matter of following the Jacobsen technique or working with a machine until we get our muscular relaxation under control or learn to drift into Alpha brain waves.

Taking it easy can sometimes be a matter of changing our whole tempo of life: just plain slowing down.

Try it some day soon, and for a full day do everything more slowly. For many of us this is very difficult, because we're used to fast-paced schedules from the time our alarm rings in the morning until we're through work and on our way home and often until we go to bed again at night. We work or play fast and hard.

If I've been able to get anything across at all in the preceding sections on relaxation, I hope I've been able to show that such a pace is perfectly consistent with relaxation. The essence of achievement is being able to relax while moving ahead and accomplishing things.

Relax and Work Too

Now I'd like to go a step further, because there are times when a slow, easy, happy, relaxed day should be your primary purpose. How do you do this? Start with that alarm in the morning. Set it earlier than usual so that you have the time to relax in all your activities, at least until you get to work. If you do this on the week end, it may be that you can arrange your social schedule so that you can have the kind of relaxed, easy day I'm going to describe all the way through.

Your Day

When your alarm wakes you up, don't get up right away. Plan just what you're going to do and plan to do it much slower than usual. Brush your teeth more slowly, dress more slowly, walk or jog a little more slowly, by all means eat more slowly. Try doing almost everything you can in slow, easy motion.

Do your best to make this slowness not a matter of restraint but a matter of letting go. A matter of easing into your activity. A matter of not letting your activity pull you ahead too fast. A matter of floating along.

Slowness is one element of this relaxed day you are going to enjoy, but that's only one part. The second part is gentleness. Resolve that every association and contact you make with everyone—your spouse, your friends, your kids, your office associates, absolutely everyone—is going to be gentle and tender.

Try a Little Tenderness

As Frank Sinatra suggests in that beautiful and gentle love song, "Try a Little Tenderness." Really try it. Be as gentle and tender and easygoing as you can be. Touch your spouse gently, tenderly, softly. Speak softly to your children and friends and the people you work with in your office or at the shop.

Above all, be gentle and tender with yourself. Don't compete. For this one day—don't compete. That's a lot easier said than done for those of us who are highly competitive. But if you feel someone coming up from behind who is walking a little faster than you are, let him go. Let him go right on by you. If you find yourself in an argument at home or at work, join the opposition or just ease off or just compliment the opposition on the point they're making. Just let them win.

Make this a day of fun. Laugh at everything you can think of. Smile at your spouse the first chance you get in the morning, whether you feel like it or not. At first you may have to force that smile. But you'll find it easier and easier as you gentle and float into the day. Smile at your children and laugh with them when you get a chance. Smile and chuckle and laugh at everyone you see on the way to work. Smile at strangers and if you can force yourself to say hi, with a smile, or hello or have a great day—do it!

Reminders

Follow through during the day with reminders to slow down, let go, smile, be soft and gentle. You may find yourself lapsing back into habits of competition, speed, driving, and there will be times when you simply have to do that because the tasks of the day demand it. But see if you can tailor those tasks to gentleness, humor, relaxation, and a slower pace. Listen more, talk less. You'll be surprised how often you can do all this and how easy it is. Follow through with luncheon—eating slowly and enjoying it, tasting each bite, sipping your beverage very slowly, taking just as long to eat as time will permit. For this one day take as much time as you can to walk, and by walking I mean amble to and from lunch, enjoying the slowness and drift of your walk.

Throughout the day come back to this slow, easy, relaxed, smiling, laughing pace as often as you can. You'll find yourself moving away from it as habit takes you away. But keep coming back. When you go home at the end of the day don't worry about missing your usual train or ride or getting home as fast as usual. Let the other fellow get ahead. Warn your wife or husband that you'll be a little late getting home.

Follow through in the evening by eating more slowly, laughing with the kids, being easy and gentle and caressing with your spouse. Have just as slow and pleasant a day as you can.

Change of Pace

I don't mean that this kind of day should become a habit, but as an occasional change of pace I think it can not only be absolutely delightful, it can also be a great way to take a vacation without going on a vacation.

Indeed, if you are starting on your vacation, this is a delightful way to do it. And if you stay with it during your vacation you will come back truly refreshed. You will be rested, a happier person, and above all a person who has given a great deal more happiness than you usually do.

Slow-Motion

Life is short, and the older we get the shorter we realize it is.

Certainly one way of enjoying it far more fully is to slow it down. And just think what that means. That we can slow down life. That we can actually move in slow-motion. That we can enjoy it and savor it and taste it and reflect on it. We can become gentle and tender and loving. We can smile and laugh and indeed make life a ball.

Nothing here should negate the great importance of learning the technique of physically relaxing, of relaxing all your muscles, of letting your mind drift and ease out of the tense, frustrating thoughts of sex and ego. Those relaxing techniques are absolutely essential. But having learned them, you now want to practice them and put them in the context of your entire day—to ease up, slow down, laugh.

Exercise Too

None of this is inconsistent with vigorous exercising. You can jog gently but fast enough to give you an aerobic training effect. It's all in the mind. When you run you don't drive your foot down hard on the ground, you let it go so that it falls gently and let your momentum push you along. If your running becomes labored, try walking. You can walk very fast and still be relaxed, if you're in good condition and if you have walked a great deal. It's a matter of putting your mind in neutral, forcing yourself to move fast but at the same time relaxing your mind so your thoughts float easily, your arms swing easily and limply at your sides, and perhaps your pace is just a shade off its usual speed. Certainly it must be slow enough and gentle enough so that you are as relaxed as you can get and remain in motion.

And Posture

The essence of good posture is grace and grace simply can't be achieved without the ease of relaxation—head erect, shoulders back, chest out, stomach in, pelvis tucked in, stand tall. You can do all of this slowly and gently, yes, easily and relaxed.

If it is a great deal easier for you not to do something like this—for instance, if pushing your shoulders back does strain a little, if your stomach wants to go out and your chest in, if you don't want to stand quite as tall as usual—well, then let go and don't quite make it. The important thing for this day, your relaxing day, your happiness day, should be that this is a day of rest, relaxation, ease, and fun. So for this one day don't strain the muscles. You can be healthier and happier as well as stronger if you do your best to maintain that good posture while at the same time reconciling it with a relaxed and easy approach to the day, but "take it easy" is the keynote.

Think It Over

Finally, at the end of the day, recollect what you have done during this day—the effect you've had on your spouse, on your children, on your associates at work, on your friends, and also how you feel. Don't you feel a little less tense, more relaxed, perhaps a little readier to go to sleep but at the same time not nearly as tired as usual?

Hasn't it been a better day? The message of this book is that there is nothing inconsistent with having this kind of day, in fact, having this kind of a happy life, while at the same time making a driving, disciplined effort to get things done.

VIII· PUTTING IT ALL TOGETHER

33 · Results and Other Tips

Now LET'S put all this together. Suppose you engage in a simultaneous exercise, diet, and relaxation program. You don't have to do this to get benefit from this book, but suppose you do. How will all this affect your health, appearance, disposition, and personality? What are the problems involved in this triple-header approach?

Well, in general, the benefits are greatly enhanced but the cost is definitely more.

Let's take a look at it step by step and see how it appeals to you.

What's Right About It?

This kind of comprehensive program, in which you engage in prolonged exercise, eat a balanced diet that keeps your weight down, and follow a systematic system of relaxation, will increase your vitality. There's no question about it. Primarily this will be the result of your exercise. Diet and relaxation will contribute, but not as much as exercise. Your general feeling of well-being will be enhanced. Exercise is the principal contributor, but diet and relaxation will help.

I can testify, based on my own experience, that your periods of spontaneous exuberance certainly increase, and the periods of depression significantly diminish, thanks largely to exercise but reinforced by relaxation.

If anything can increase your longevity, I think this kind

of program should make an important contribution. Exercise, diet, and relaxation are all of major importance in maintaining good health and a sound body.

Once again I should point out that any exercise program should be a regular program. Exercise that is spasmodic and irregular can be dangerous. And before engaging in unaccustomed exercise everyone should have a thorough checkup by a physician. But if you are careful to guard against problems, the three-part combination should give you a new lease on life.

Certainly all three of these programs will contribute directly to reducing the likelihood of heart attacks, stroke, and the general debility that obesity causes in older people.

One thing to remember about this program is that there is often a lag factor and you may have to wait months before major dividends come in. But if you continue, the desired benefits are inevitable, provided you maintain these programs on a regular, daily basis.

A Slim New You

How does the combined Proxmire program affect your appearance? First of all, you'll soon be lean and vital-looking if you follow it on a day-to-day basis. Anyone who does vigorous exercise of the kind suggested here, eats moderately, and learns to relax thoroughly will be in enviable shape in a short time, and will stay that way.

Your color and skin tone will improve. Your whole physical appearance will take on a look of exuberant good health. There doesn't seem to be any question that when you are healthy and vital you look the same way. And when you are relaxed you look happier and better.

The Price You Pay

Naturally, any program of this kind takes time. But with careful planning you can work it fairly easily into your day, and you'll find that it adds to your energy. Anyone can manage to fit it in by settling for a little less sleep, a little less loafing and TV watching, and perhaps even a little less social life. If you follow a program regularly you'll soon find that the rewards make up for these sacrifices.

Some people may be bored when they first attempt a half-hour of exercise and a half-hour of learning relaxation every day. That's a full hour out of your waking day. However, most people find as time goes on that they are enjoying that hour. It can be exhilarating and exciting.

Perhaps the toughest requirement of this kind of triple program is the everyday discipline. It's one thing to diet, but it's quite another to combine a diet with vigorous exercise and systematic relaxation. To do all three and do them every day and do them indefinitely does require discipline, but I find that the disciplines reinforce each other, especially if you can work out your schedule so you do the same activity every day at the same time and then stick with it regardless.

Not everyone you know is going to congratulate you for undertaking this program. Some people may call you an exercise nut, a diet nut, and a yogi nut, or they may say you've become too antisocial and self-centered in your pre-occupation with self-improvement. Only a few, probably very few, will react that way, and it shouldn't bother you since you're doing this for yourself. You'll find that most people are delighted with the new you. After all, you are more pleasant, more attractive, healthier, happier. So what's wrong with that?

Vastly Improve Your Chances

The main point I'd like to make here is that almost anyone who begins with only an average constitution and who is not necessarily blessed with exceptionally healthy ancestors can achieve a level of vital, energetic, almost disease-free life, with a good chance at living a long time, if he consciously follows the planned program of exercise, relaxation, and diet even to a limited and moderate extent.

It's important to remember that nothing, but nothing, can guarantee a long life or a life free of disease, even of heart disease. But you can guarantee a far better chance that your life will be freer of disease, probably longer, and certainly more vital and energetic.

Follow the Proxmire program and you will be rated by the professional handicappers as having a far, far greater chance to achieve good health. By and large, good health is a matter of being free from debilitating diseases. And as we know, those diseases, with the exception of tuberculosis, have not been reduced. The incidence is growing. Heart disease and stroke have become epidemic because of our self-indulgent and tense existence.

One interesting and significant side effect I can absolutely guarantee is that you will have a more orderly life, that you will strengthen your will power to control your life not only with respect to health but with respect to your job and your goals. You will enhance your capacity to organize and direct your life and get the things you want.

If you take the painful steps to train your body to be healthy, then you can take those similar painful steps to discipline your mind so that you can read, write, speak, and listen with far more assurance and effectiveness.

You can apply the same principle of self-control and self-direction to achieve a variety of goals.

Good Health and Mental Competence

In a sense the achievement of good health is not much different from the development of a strong intellectual capability. With some work toward these goals, we can achieve a far higher level of accomplishment than if we simply depended on our untrained native abilities.

This is my point on health. The fact that we all know

many healthy, long-lived people who don't work at it certainly shouldn't convince you that a planned regimen isn't necessary. For most of us, to be healthy we have to work at it. We have to work at it every day. We have to think about it, plan it, and stick to our plan.

You can achieve good health with all its blessings through conscious, conscientious, day-after-day effort. And if you understand it, if you think about it, if you realize fully the implications of lassitude and self-indulgence, you are very likely to take corrective action.

That's why I wrote this book.

34 · Winston Churchill—an Exception That Proves the Rule

HOW DOES ONE EXPLAIN a man like Winston Churchill? No man in recent years accomplished more or led a more conspicuously self-indulgent life. He was obese, a notorious overeater, an excessive drinker, a slugabed who liked to stay in bed during most of the daylight hours. He seemed to lead a rollicking, boisterous, full, happy, as well as enormously constructive life. How about Churchill?

Well, let's consider it. One of the few men of our time whom we can classify as a statesman—there probably aren't more than four or five—Churchill was truly exceptional. He was exceptional not only because of his magnificent role in meeting the most terrible challenge modern England has faced, but also because of his amazing eloquence and brilliance, the speeches he delivered, the books he wrote, and the constant wit and humor as well as strength and courage that he brought to the crisis of World War II.

The turning point of World War II may well have been the Battle of Britain, and the voice that rallied that gallant country, that inspired this country to support the Allies to victory, was very largely that of Winston Churchill.

What a great man! What a great personality and what a varied talent, not only as a leader and speaker and writer but as a painter and philosopher. He met our greatest modern threat, the challenge of Fascist aggression, and more than any other man brought the free world through.

Achievements Late in Life

The astonishing physical fact about Winston Churchill is not only that he was a self-indulgent, heavy drinker and an immense eater, but that he achieved his greatest distinction and was at the peak of his immense power and talent in his sixties.

Winston Churchill was sixty-two at the peak of the Battle of Britain and he went on with his leadership, his eloquence, and his humor, for years and years after that.

I can remember my father-in-law saying how he looked forward to having Winston Churchill come to this country to make his Fulton, Missouri, Iron Curtain speech. It seemed clear that because of his age and his physical condition this was probably the last time Churchill would be able to travel outside of England. We were fortunate to be the country he would visit. We would have an actual chance to hear Winston Churchill himself speak. My father-in-law, who was reasonably lean and moderate in his habits, died at the age of fifty-seven, long before Sir Winston expired in the fullness of his great life at the age of ninety.

How does one explain this? There is no easy answer. Indeed, there may be no answer. It's always possible that you can eat and drink as much as you want and exercise only when the spirit urges you and you will still end up a Churchill.

The fact is that by neglecting or abusing your health you probably won't have any significant effect one way or the other on your personality or your intelligence. You may if you are very fortunate live a long time. But you'll have to be one of the truly rare ones if you are obese. You *may* lead a reasonably healthy, comfortable life in your advanced years but you will be a rare one indeed. And if you think Churchill led a healthy and happy life in his advanced years, you are absolutely wrong.

Consider what Churchill's doctors said about his declining years. They were almost incredibly miserable.

Churchill's Last Years

Churchill suffered constant discomfort and agonies of pain during his seventies and eighties. He once described himself as nothing but a breathing, excreting misery.

All of us remember his inspiring personality and great wit, and most of us associate that inspiration and wit with a comfortable, happy spirit. But Churchill's last years poignantly dramatize how life can be worse than death for a sedentary, obese, very old man. The extraordinary diary of Churchill's personal physician, Lord Moran of Manton, notes that on December 28, 1955, when Churchill still had ten years to live, "Winston was looking very glum. 'I'm waiting about for death,' he said soberly. There was a long pause while he stared in front of him. 'But it won't come.'"

And Lord Moran wrote of the last ten years of Churchill's life:

> As the years went by, he gave up reading. He seldom spoke and did not seem to know his friends. We would rise to our feet as he came into the room, supported by his nurses. As they pushed him to his chair his feet made a slapping sound on the floor. Very small, almost shrunken, he appeared huddled up in the depths of a big chair. There he sat through the afternoon hours, staring into the fire, giving it a prod with his stick when the room felt cold.
>
> If in those sad years of mounting decrepitude, he seemed to be fearful of the future of mankind and grew to hate change and become intolerant of criticism; if he did not try to hide his distaste for what was left to him of life, I cannot forget the anguish of that time when, as the biographer Lord Rosebery said of Winston's father, "He was the chief mourner at his own protracted funeral."

Churchill had more of the external joys of old age than any man of this century. What a glorious figure of courage, wisdom, wit he had been! And what rare vindication of his great career his later years brought him. He possessed wealth, superb medical attention, a loving and devoted wife.

It can truly be said that he had literally everything to make his last years pure gold except for one humble blessing: good health. And without health everything turned to bitter ashes. For those who point to Churchill as the prime example of how obesity and self-indulgence can still permit a long and glorious life, I say, Look a little closer. Churchill's life proves precisely the opposite.

The chances are that you will live a longer life and a far happier, more exuberant, stronger life if you make the extraordinary effort of developing an exercise program and disciplining yourself to the far more extraordinary extent of staying with that kind of program for the rest of your life, and if you combine this with a moderate eating program and regular sessions of relaxation.

Health Isn't Everything

Just one more observation with respect to Churchill. Health is a great thing. It is one of the greatest blessings we can have in life. But let's face it, it isn't the greatest blessing.

Winston Churchill brought a towering will and talent to the service of his country in dealing with the great international crisis of the twentieth century. His health was irrelevant to it. Considering Churchill's story should remind us that, critical as health is to life and achievement, there are certainly other considerations that are more important.

Eager as I am for support of my program, I have to acknowledge that health is not all. It isn't as important as love or honesty or courage.

35 · Your Lifetime Commitment

MANY MILLIONS of Americans have become ecologists and have become conscious of their responsibility for their environment. It's a wonderful new development because it's concerned not only with keeping our own property clean and attractive but doing our best to make our country a cleaner, more wholesome place.

And the Congress is working constantly to pass legislation to clean up water and air at an immense cost to taxpayers and industry. This is a highly controversial issue because of the great economic sacrifice that cleaner environment requires of even this affluent country.

Human Ecology

At the same time there has been only a whisper of a suggestion that there is such a thing as human ecology. And by that I mean your responsibility for your own system, not merely for your own property but for yourself.

How ridiculous it is to have people who are habitual smokers talk about air pollution! The air pollution they impose on their own bodies is infinitely more damaging if they smoke regularly than the air pollution that has become the bane of our cities.

Don't get me wrong, I believe deeply in ecology and our responsibility for a better, cleaner environment. This is something that is going to take many, many years and probably many generations, and it's something that cannot be within the control of any one person or even any group of people.

But the ecology of your own body is almost completely within your own control. The chances are overwhelming that you can have a sound, healthy, strong body, be able to withstand stress and meet crisis, and be able to contribute to a better life for others.

Most of us as parents are conscious of our responsibility to our children and are very anxious to inculcate healthy habits in them. Few of us take the time to realize that the best way we can do this is to set an example for our children by adopting healthy habits ourselves and in the process enormously improve the quality of our own lives.

The Quality of Your Life

The quality of life has been a developing slogan of this generation. People talk about how economic progress has meant a retrogression in our environment and to a considerable extent they're right. Well, how about the quality of your own life, your own personal life? It depends above all on what you eat and how much, on what exercise you take and how much, on your capacity to control your emotions, your fantasies, your muscular tension. You and you alone in this free country of ours have complete, total, sovereign control of your body. This is true even if you are a child and your mother and father tell you what you can eat or not eat and how you should exercise. This is a decision that ultimately you make and the wise parent will recognize that you should make it on the basis of persuasion and example if you are going to be strong and independent and a free citizen.

For these reasons I'm not talking simply about a temporary approach to getting in shape for a little while, I'm talking about a permanent way of life.

Forever

This book will have given you no benefit at all if you feel it's simply useful for losing weight over a few days or even months. It must be a lifetime commitment. But life can be long, happy, full of exuberant strength, if you commit yourself to a program of dieting and relaxing of the kind I suggest.

No, I'm not asking you to be an absolute paragon. I don't expect you, any more than I expect my children, any more than I expect myself, to be at the ideal weight, to develop the ideal amount of strength, to be able to be completely relaxed physically and mentally on signal.

But you can set reasonable goals. If you determine what weight you really want to be, think about it, consider it, discuss it with your doctor, your wife or husband, your friends, you will arrive at it. You can do it and you can stay with it all the days of your life. If you decide that you are going to develop your physical stamina by a vigorous, long daily walk or run or swim—you can do it. And you can do it not this year or next year, but forever.

You can also learn to control your tension. Tensions may have made you irritable, given you headaches, increased your blood pressure, aggravated any number of illnesses including heart disease. But you can learn to turn that off, let it go, allow it to drift away, if you have the sense of discipline and commitment to do so.

Physical-Fitness Program: a Shame

As a United States Senator, I'm convinced that the so-called physical fitness program of this country is a national disgrace. Just how pitiful our physical-fitness programs are is dramatized by the remarkably small resources our federal and state governments devote to them.

In all fairness, the federal program has sharply increased in the past two years, but the increase has been from almost nothing to little more than that.

This country now expends some seventy-five billion dollars every year to treat its illnesses. That comes to about three hundred seventy-five dollars for every person every year in the United States. Many of these billions are provided through various federal "health" programs, including Medicare and Medicaid. Billions more are provided by the states.

By contrast the federal government's physical-fitness program—designed to *prevent* illnesses—now has exactly twelve people in it, including secretarial personnel. The resources the federal government devotes to physical fitness literally amount to a fraction of a cent on a per capita basis. And the states are even more negligent. Forty-three of the fifty states have absolutely no physical-fitness program whatsoever. Of the seven that go through the motions, only four provide *any* funding.

Texas has by far the biggest and best program. This amounts to one director and three staff members with a $61,000 budget (in 1972)—the princely sum of a little more than half a cent for every person in Texas. And Texas is the best!

I am very much opposed to any attempt to solve the problem of the disgracefully poor physical condition of the people of America by trying to throw money at it. In sixteen years in the United States Senate I have seen that approach lose too often. We should not appropriate additional billions or millions. We don't need to spend more money. What we do need to do is to require the National Institutes of Health and the Administrators of Medicare and Medicaid to use a small part of their swollen budgets to promote physical fitness. In this case an ounce of prevention is worth a ton of cure.

One or another national celebrity is put in charge of a so-called physical-fitness program, but nothing significant happens. Occasional, but very occasional, ads appear on television encouraging young children to engage in physical activity. That may do a little good, but precious little.

The one distinguished exception to this appalling failure of our leaders to recognize the importance of a healthy people is the recent effective and concentrated attack on tobacco. Certainly tobacco is a killer. It's responsible for a great deal of debility and disease. At considerable expense, the television industry at least has now been organized to end its enticement of people to untimely death and disease by stopping tobacco ads. Television and radio have done an excellent job of acquainting the public with the indisputable facts that the Surgeon General has found about the destructive effects of tobacco on health.

With all that is known, anyone who smokes is performing a constant ecological outrage on his own body. He's likely to die of lung cancer or heart disease.

A Nation-wide Campaign

Just imagine if all the radio stations and all the television stations and most of the newspapers in the country began to really tell Americans what rotten physical shape they are in, honestly and directly! Imagine if they told us regularly and reminded us regularly what we can do about it; if we made vigorous walking a widespread national pastime; if as much time were devoted to the benefits of a moderately balanced diet as to teasing and enticing millions of palates to consume dead food that contributes nothing to the body but obesity. Or if we could spend a little regular prime television time informing Americans about the immense benefits of being able to use self-discipline to relax.

Of course the market for aspirin, tranquilizers, and sleeping pills would diminish and with it much of the related drug culture which wreaks its devastation on the country. But that would be a side benefit. There would be an enormous increase in national energy and national health, and a mammoth saving of billions of dollars we now expend in Medicare to many Americans whose illness is simply the result of ignorance, self-indulgence, or laziness.

Why Do You Do It?

My easygoing, happy-go-lucky son Ted recently asked, "Dad, why do you subject yourself to such rigorous control? Is it worth it? Why force yourself to run when you're tired? Why follow such a strict diet? Why do you do it?"

My answer is: "Sheer physical joy and comfort and exhilaration." Without any reference to any kind of moral concept or any prospect that some day I may be stronger or live a little longer, I actually do feel better because I'm in shape. It's true that the taste buds may be denied occasionally, and it's true that physical effort is often unpleasant, but I'm positive that if you total up all the physical pleasure of actually being in shape, the feeling of well-being, the strength and health, the capacity to enjoy food and walking, sleeping and even breathing, you do come out ahead by being "hard on yourself."

Take Joe Namath, a personality who is usually viewed as pleasure-loving. He is quoted as saying that he likes training camp, with all its grim requirements for physical conditioning, because he just loves to be in shape. Joe is right. There is a very large dividend indeed: the sheer pleasure of good conditioning.

Many years ago the English philosopher Jeremy Bentham developed a set of philosophical principles which he called utilitarianism. The essence of utilitarianism is that man's actions in life are designed to maximize his pleasures and minimize his pains. Of course pleasure is defined in the broadest sense, including the enjoyment that one gets from spiritual experiences and altruistic action such as charitable donation or participation. In this very broad sense many are utilitarians. Judging life from the Jeremy Bentham notion of making it as pleasant and pleasurable as can be, discipline, sacrifice, effort can win a pay-off in the sheer physical enjoyment of well-being. Dieting and relaxation are well worth it. I'll argue that with the laziest, fattest, most undisciplined sophist you can find.

Like a Monk?

Some will say that in order to follow the Proxmire program it is necessary to live like a monk, that you have to deprive yourself of so many things it just isn't worthwhile.

My answer is loud, clear, emphatic: No indeed! You will develop the capacity to generate exuberance spontaneously, you will laugh more, and get up in the morning looking eagerly ahead to a day of solid, genuine physical enjoyment. You will enjoy food more than ever. Furthermore, there is absolutely nothing you cannot eat on the Proxmire proposal. You can eat ice cream, peanuts, butter, gravy, whatever turns you on. The only suggestion is that you balance your diet and exert some hold-down on fatty foods and foods that are likely to cause cholesterol. Above all, you should make friends with three things:

1. Your scale.
2. Your calorie counter.
3. Vigorous exercise to burn a great many more calories.

Consider my proposed exercise routine. If you take a strenuous five-mile walk every day, you can eat everything you eat now and you will lose. You will enjoy your food more, too.

And certainly no one can say that learning how to relax is living like a monk. After all, you are not imposing deprivation on your body for the sake of your spirit. You are enhancing your physical joys. Relaxation makes life more pleasant. It makes you a happier, warmer, gentler person. You can love better not only in the physical sense but in a social and companionable sense too, because you've conquered your tensions, directed your ambitions and your drive.

Alcohol? It's Up to You

I've said nothing favorable about consuming alcoholic beverages because I believe that alcoholic beverages even in moderation have an adverse affect on health. Nevertheless, probably a majority of our adult citizens do consume them, so let's look at it this way: If you're going to drink you're far better off if you also exercise, follow a sensible diet, and know how to relax. I think you'll be better off if you don't drink, but that's just a personal opinion which many, many people will contradict. However, everyone agrees that you're far better off if your drinking is moderate.

Any Part Will Help

I would like to say just once more that you don't have to adopt the total Proxmire program. You'll benefit if you adopt any part of it. This means that you can benefit if you simply walk vigorously two or three miles a day and change nothing else, or if you decide to do nothing about diet or exercise but to follow a systematic but limited relaxation program.

You can tailor the program to be sure that the goals you adopt and commit yourself to are realistic and limited. There's nothing in the world to prevent you from reappraising those goals and setting them a little bit higher as the months and years go by and you decide you can do a little better.

If you want to improve your physical fitness, your health, your personality, your disposition, you can do it and you can do it to the extent that you wish.

My father used to tell me that you get out of life just what you put into it, a cliché that too many of us too easily dismiss. We dismiss it because we know that, being human, we will not put into it as much as our conscience tells us we should.

Try a little. Maybe a very little at the beginning. As time goes on you will find that you can do better.